# The History of
# the T.U.C. 1868-1968

# THE HISTORY OF THE T.U.C. 1868-1968 A PICTORIAL SURVEY OF A SOCIAL REVOLUTION

*Editor: Lionel Birch; picture research by Doris Bryen; cover design by The Hamlyn Group; and additional research and assistance from the staff of the Trades Union Congress.*

*Published by the General Council of the Trades Union Congress, Congress House, Great Russell Street, London, W.C.1.* © 1968.

*Distributed throughout the world by The Hamlyn Publishing Group Limited, The Centre, Feltham, Middlesex.*

*Printed photo-offset by Sanders Phillips and Company, at the Baynard Press, Northampton Road, London, E.C.1.*

# Foreword

THIS BOOK shows how a small debating assembly grew into the national representative body of British trade unionism, sharing in the making of government policies, taking part in administering major social services and meeting on equal terms with the spokesmen of the nation's employers. In the course of that evolution the T.U.C. has been instrumental in provoking crucial developments in the structure and purposes of British governments, a radical transformation of British society and fundamental changes in the structure of British industry.

Intended to be a forum where trade unionists could discuss their common problems and a shop window for trade unionism, the annual Trades Union Congress soon became a focus for the views of working people about all the questions affecting their working lives. Britain's workers made the T.U.C. the vehicle by which their views could be conveyed to Ministers. Slowly the T.U.C. gained competence in articulating those views; slowly and hesitantly, though speeded intermittently by the urgencies of two world wars, governments recognised the essential contribution which the T.U.C. could bring to the conduct of national affairs, by reason of its capacity to represent the collective industrial experience of working people and to apply that experience realistically in the resolution of national industrial, economic and social questions. Slowly and hesitantly, too, employers similarly accepted the T.U.C.'s right and competence in industrial affairs.

The T.U.C.'s assertion of a right to share in the government of the nation inevitably involved an obligation to assume some share of responsibility in implementing policies agreed with governments; and the fulfilment of this obligation equally inevitably tests the T.U.C.'s representative capacity. Created and sustained by autonomous trade unions to serve their common national interests and precluded by its nature from the exercise of executive power, the T.U.C. has been compelled, in order to perform the tasks which unions have placed upon it, to develop an unequalled capacity for leadership by consent. Gradually, and sometimes painfully, despite setbacks and disappointments, by patient and unspectacular resource and practical good sense, it has gained the respect and loyalty of unions to an extent which permits it to act effectively on their collective behalf. As governmental policies encroach increasingly, at the demand of trade unionists, upon the conduct of industrial affairs, and in so doing intrude into matters within the domestic autonomy of unions, the T.U.C.'s proper acceptance of a share of responsibility in those policies tests its capacity for leadership as it enters its second century more severely than at any time since 1926.

The T.U.C. and its affiliated trade unions form a single entity. But the history of the T.U.C., while embracing in the past hundred years the development of trade unionism in Great Britain, is something more than the sum of the histories of its constituent trade unions. This book describes the origins and growth of the T.U.C.'s unique contribution to British trade unionism and to the creation of modern Britain.

_George Woodcock._

# Members of the Trades Union Congress General Council 1967-68

CHAIRMAN

Lord Wright, C.B.E. ................ *Amalgamated Weavers' Association*

VICE-CHAIRMAN

Lord Collison, C.B.E. ............... *National Union of Agricultural Workers*

GENERAL COUNCIL

| | |
|---|---|
| Mr. A. W. Allen, C.B.E. ............. | *Union of Shop, Distributive & Allied Workers* |
| Mr. W. C. Anderson, C.B.E. ....... | *National & Local Government Officers' Association* |
| Miss W. Baddeley.................... | *Amalgamated Engineering Union* |
| Mr. D. Basnett ....................... | *National Union of General & Municipal Workers* |
| Mr. J. G. Bothwell, O.B.E. ......... | *Transport Salaried Staffs' Association* (resigned in January, 1968, because of ill-health) |
| Mr. J. M. Boyd....................... | *Amalgamated Engineering Union* |
| Mr. R. W. Briginshaw............... | *Society of Graphical & Allied Trades* |
| Mr. L. Cannon·...................... | *Electrical Trades Union* |
| Lord Carron ......................... | *Amalgamated Engineering Union* |
| Lord Cooper ....,.................... | *National Union of General & Municipal Workers* |
| The Rt. Hon. F. Cousins............ | *Transport & General Workers' Union* |
| Mr. J. Crawford ..................... | *National Association of Colliery Overmen, Deputies & Shotfirers* |
| Mr. D. H. Davies.................... | *Iron & Steel Trades Confederation* |
| Sir Sidney Ford, M.B.E............... | *National Union of Mineworkers* |
| Mr. S. F. Greene, C.B.E............. | *National Union of Railwaymen* |
| Mr. A. E. Griffiths .................. | *Associated Society of Locomotive Engineers & Firemen* |
| Mr. F. Hayday, C.B.E. .............. | *National Union of General & Municipal Workers* |
| Mr. E. Haynes....................... | *Bakers' Union* |
| Mr. S. Hill, O.B.E. .................. | *National Union of Public Employees* |
| Mr. W. Hogarth ..................... | *National Union of Seamen* |
| Mr. T. Jackson ...................... | *Union of Post Office Workers* |
| Mr. J. W. Jones ..................... | *Transport & General Workers' Union* |
| Mr. G. H. Lowthian, C.B.E......... | *Amalgamated Union of Building Trade Workers* |
| Mr. A. Martin........................ | *National Union of Mineworkers* |
| Mr. D. McGarvey ................... | *Amalgamated Society of Boilermakers, Shipwrights, Blacksmiths & Structural Workers* |
| Mr. J. E. Newton .................... | *National Union of Tailors & Garment Workers* |
| Sir Tom O'Brien ..................... | *National Association of Theatrical & Kine Employees* |
| Mrs. C. M. Patterson............... | *Transport & General Workers' Union* |
| Mr. J. A. Peel ....................... | *National Union of Dyers, Bleachers & Textile Workers* |
| Mr. C. T. H. Plant, O.B.E. ......... | *Inland Revenue Staff Federation* |
| Mr. A. Roberts...................... | *National Union of Vehicle Builders* |
| Mr. S. A. Robinson ................. | *National Union of Boot & Shoe Operatives* |
| Mr. G. F. Smith ..................... | *Amalgamated Society of Woodworkers* |

GENERAL SECRETARY

The Rt. Hon. George Woodcock, C.B.E.

ASSISTANT GENERAL SECRETARY

Mr. Victor Feather, C.B.E.

# Contents

# PROPOSED CONGRESS OF TRADES COUNCILS

AND OTHER

## Federations of Trades Societies.

———— ⟡ ————

MANCHESTER, FEBRUARY 21st. 1868.

FELLOW-UNIONISTS,

The Manchester and Salford Trades Council having recently taken into their serious consideration the present aspect of Trades Unions, and the profound ignorance which prevails in the public mind with reference to their operations and principles, together with the probability of an attempt being made by the Legislature, during the present session of Parliament, to introduce a measure detrimental to the interests of such Societies, beg most respectfully to suggest the propriety of holding in Manchester, as the main centre of industry in the provinces, a Congress of the Representatives of Trades Councils and other similar Federations of Trades Societies. By confining the Congress to such bodies it is conceived that a deal of expense will be saved, as Trades will thus be represented collectively; whilst there will be a better opportunity afforded of selecting the most intelligent and efficient exponents of our principles.

It is proposed that the Congress shall assume the character of the annual meetings of the British Association for the Advancement of Science and the Social Science Association, in the transactions of which Societies the artizan class are almost entirely excluded; and that papers, previously carefully prepared, shall be laid before the Congress on the various subjects which at the present time affect Trades Societies, each paper to be followed by discussion upon the points advanced, with a view of the merits and demerits of each question being thoroughly ventilated through the medium of the public press. It is further suggested that the subjects treated upon shall include the following :—

1.—Trades Unions an absolute necessity.
2.—Trades Unions and Political Economy.
3.—The Effect of Trades Unions on Foreign Competition.
4.—Regulation of the Hours of Labour.
5.—Limitation of Apprentices.
6.—Technical Education.
7.—Arbitration and Courts of Conciliation.
8.—Co-operation.
9.—The present Inequality of the Law in regard to Conspiracy, Intimidation, Picketing, Coercion, &c.
10.—Factory Acts Extension Bill, 1867: the necessity of Compulsory Inspection, and its application to all places where Women and Children are employed.
11.—The present Royal Commission on Trades Unions: how far worthy of the confidence of the Trades Union interest.
12.—The necessity of an Annual Congress of Trade Representatives from the various centres of industry.

All Trades Councils and other Federations of Trades are respectfully solicited to intimate their adhesion to this project on or before the 6th of April next, together with a notification of the subject of the paper that each body will undertake to prepare; after which date all information as to place of meeting, &c., will be supplied.

It is also proposed that the Congress be held on the 4th of May next, and that all liabilities in connection therewith shall not extend beyond its sittings.

Communications to be addressed to MR. W. H. WOOD, Typographical Institute, 29, Water Street, Manchester,

By order of the Manchester and Salford Trades Council,

S. C. NICHOLSON, PRESIDENT.
W. H. WOOD, SECRETARY.

# The first Trades Union Congress —and the men who brought it to birth

THE WORDS were those of Samuel Caldwell Nicholson, President of the Manchester and Salford Trades Council, who, with William Henry Wood, secretary of the trades council, was later to send out the first summons to the first Trades Union Congress; a circular which is reproduced on page 10.

Both men were journeymen compositors. Nicholson was treasurer, and Wood was secretary of the Manchester Typographical Society. Nicholson's momentous words were uttered on the spur of the moment, after he had heard from a brother compositor, William Dronfield, secretary of the Sheffield Typographical Society, an account of his frustrated and stultifying attempts to obtain a wide hearing for the trade union point of view through the medium of the Congress of the National Association for the Promotion of Social Science.

The Social Science Association, as this middle-class body was commonly called, had for several years professed a sympathetic interest in trade unionism. Yet when, at the Association's Ninth Annual Congress, held in October 1865, Dronfield read a paper in defence of trade unions—after a ferocious attack on them by the previous speaker—not one word of Dronfield's paper, nor of the ensuing discussion in which a number of Sheffield trade unionists took part, was ever allowed to appear in the Association's report.

What then was the point, Dronfield pondered, of trade unionists going to these congresses of allegedly "progressive" middle-class organisations, if the views of working men present were to be methodically suppressed? And from Nicholson came the epoch-making answer: "Why not have a congress of our own?"

Why not? There were other good and urgent reasons for the establishment of such a congress at such a time. Thus far, throughout the 1860s, the trades unions had had their backs to the wall. The Hornby *v.* Close judgment had deprived them of legal protection for their funds. The trade slump of 1866 had given the press a pretext to denounce British unions for unpatriotically undermining Britain's trading position in the face of low-wage competition from "furriners". The "Sheffield outrages", perpetrated by a handful of extremists against non-unionists, had been publicised in a manner designed further to inflame public opinion. Employers in Sheffield and elsewhere had developed the lock-out as a made-to-measure instrument for the disintegration of trade societies. And, early in 1867, the Government had appointed a Royal Commission of Inquiry into Trade Unions, whose eventual findings, it was feared, might put the clock back to 1824, when all trade combinations had been quite simply illegal.

Confronted by these recurrent onslaughts and by the menacing uncertainties of the immediate future, individual trade unions found themselves struggling on in vulnerable isolation, with no national representative body through which they could hope to speak and act in unison.

True, as far back as the early 1830s Robert Owen and John Doherty had organised their own kind of national trades' conference; but this had borne no lasting fruit. And the National Association of United Trades for the Protection of Labour, which was founded in 1845, had failed to win the essential participation of most of the larger societies, who were preoccupied with their own individual trades and did not care for the idea of trades' federations or "general unions".

In fact, such wider inter-trades leadership of the working-class movement as existed in the years before the first Trades Union Congress was vested in the trades councils. Of these, the most influential was the London Trades Council, which had come into being after the London builders' strike over the nine-hour day, in 1860. This trades council was guided by men like Robert Applegarth, general secretary of the carpenters and joiners, a national amalgamated society; William Allan of the engineers, another national amalgamated society; and George Odger, an official of the ladies' shoemakers. These men, and a few other of their colleagues, were later to be given the name of the "Junta" by Sidney and Beatrice Webb, who described them as "an informal cabinet of the trade union world".

The London Junta in the 1860s pursued a cautious and conciliatory policy where strikes and lockouts were concerned, but at the same time they led some vigorous campaigning for various political reforms, such as the right of the working man to vote; and they pressed for new legislation to regulate conditions in the mines, and for a Conciliation and Arbitration Act. They also backed the Glasgow Trades Council's energetic campaign for the reform of the Master and Servant Act, which made it possible for magistrates to threaten strikers with imprisonment for breach of contract, if they did not return to work.

In February 1866, following a lock-out in the Sheffield file trades, the Sheffield Association of Organised Trades, of which William Dronfield was secretary, sent out an invitation to all national " trades " and trades councils in the country to attend a conference of trades' delegates with the object of creating "a national organisation among the trades of the United Kingdom, for the purpose of effectually resisting all lock-outs".

In July 1866, 138 delegates, representing some 200,000 members, did attend this Sheffield conference, which, as William Dronfield remarked seven years later, "laid the foundations of the annual trades congresses".

But soon after the appointment of a Royal Commission of Inquiry into Trade Unions was announced, in February 1867, it emerged that two rival bodies were aiming to present the trade union case to the Commission, as self-appointed representatives of the whole Movement. On the one hand, the Junta-dominated Committee of Amalgamated Trades; on the other, the St. Martin's Hall Conference-Committee, so called after the conference of trades council and trade union delegates convened there in March 1867 by the London Working Men's Association, under the leadership of George Potter, whose militant policies in industrial disputes had antagonised the wary members of the Junta.

Two rival ad hoc committees, but no single genuinely representative permanent body had yet been elected or delegated to speak with one voice for the trade unionists of the country as a whole.

So . . . "Why not have a congress of our own?"

Once the idea had struck, Nicholson and Wood lost no time in planning the Congress, which they already envisaged as destined to become an annual event. The first circular, which seems to have been despatched in February 1868, was addressed to "trades councils and other similar federations of trade societies" only. The original intention was for the Congress to be held on May 4th; but this date was later postponed until June 2nd, "in order to afford sufficient time for all the various trade organisations to send delegates and prepare papers". And then a second circular was issued, extending a wider invitation, to individual trade unions.

In the event, thirty-four delegates, representing some 118,000 trade union members, and including William Dronfield, attended this first Congress, which was held in the Mechanics' Institute, David Street, Manchester, from June 2nd to June 6th 1868. Of the thirty-four delegates, only two were London trade unionists. But one of the two was George Potter, secretary of a local London society of carpenters and joiners (which was not affiliated to Applegarth's National Society) and who edited the militant and increasingly influential labour journal called the "Bee-hive". The London Trades Council, and the Junta had decided to cold-shoulder the Manchester Congress, as seeming to be a potential rival to their own authority.

Never, perhaps, has such an historically pregnant event gone so scantily recorded. No pictorial record of the first Trades Union Congress, or of its two dedicated sponsors, Nicholson and Wood, seems to have survived. And most of the surviving written descriptions of the Congress are fragmentary. By far the best and most comprehensive of them is contained in A. E. Musson's booklet, "The Congress of 1868: The Origins and Establishment of the Trades Union Congress", published by the T.U.C. in 1955.

The overall aim of the delegates—who met under the presidency of W. H. Wood, because Samuel Nicholson had felt obliged to go to Derby to attend a meeting of the Annual Moveable Delegation of the Order of Druids, of which he was general secretary—was to consider questions of outstanding importance to trade unionists and to give publicity to those considerations. Papers were read on most of the various subjects listed in the summons to the Congress (and reprinted here on page 10). Each paper was followed by a discussion.

"The most important", writes A. E. Musson in his booklet, "were naturally those concerning the Royal Commission and the legal position of trade unions . . . the Congress expressed the 'suspicion and disfavour' with which the great majority of trade unions regarded the Royal Commission, 'both in regard to the unfair composition and also to its one-sided, and to a great extent secret, proceedings'. It pledged itself, in the name of the societies represented, 'to aid the London Committee of Amalgamated Trades in their laudable effort to secure the legal protection of trade societies' funds'. . . ."

Thus, as Musson observes, the trade union leadership was still left in the hands of the Junta.

The first Trades Union Congress further resolved "that the influence of this Congress shall be directed to aiding the London Conference of Amalgamated Trades in their endeavours . . . to amend the law in regard to conspiracy, intimidation, picketing, coercion, etc., which is . . . capable of such misconstructions that it is utterly impossible that justice can be done".

This first Congress did also pass a resolution "that it is highly desirable that the trades of the United Kingdom should hold an annual congress, for the purpose of bringing the trades into closer alliance, and to take action in all Parliamentary matters pertaining to the general interests of the working classes". And it was agreed that the next Congress should be held at Birmingham—the timing being left to the Birmingham Trades' Council.

These resolutions of the first Trades Union Congress, incidentally, set the theme of this present book's first section, which seeks to illuminate the development of the T.U.C.'s growth and activities from 1868 until the turn of the century; a period in which the T.U.C.'s principal efforts were directed—with limited and intermittent success—towards influencing successive governments to protect the trade unions as societies, and to protect the worker as an individual human being.

As Sam Woods, secretary of the Parliamentary Committee of the T.U.C. from 1894 to 1904, put it:

"Notwithstanding all the teachings of political economists, all the doctrines taught by way of supply and demand, we say there is a greater doctrine overriding all those, and that is the doctrine of humanity." ∎

# Royal Commission of Inquiry into Trade Unions: Queen Victoria enjoins...

*The letter from Queen Victoria, which enjoined Sir William Erle and his fellow members of the Royal Commission to "inquire into and report on the organisation and rules of Trades Unions and other Associations, whether of workmen or employers, and to inquire into and report on the effect produced by such Trades Unions and Associations on the workmen and employers respectively, and on the relations between workmen and employers, and on the trade and industry of the country..."*

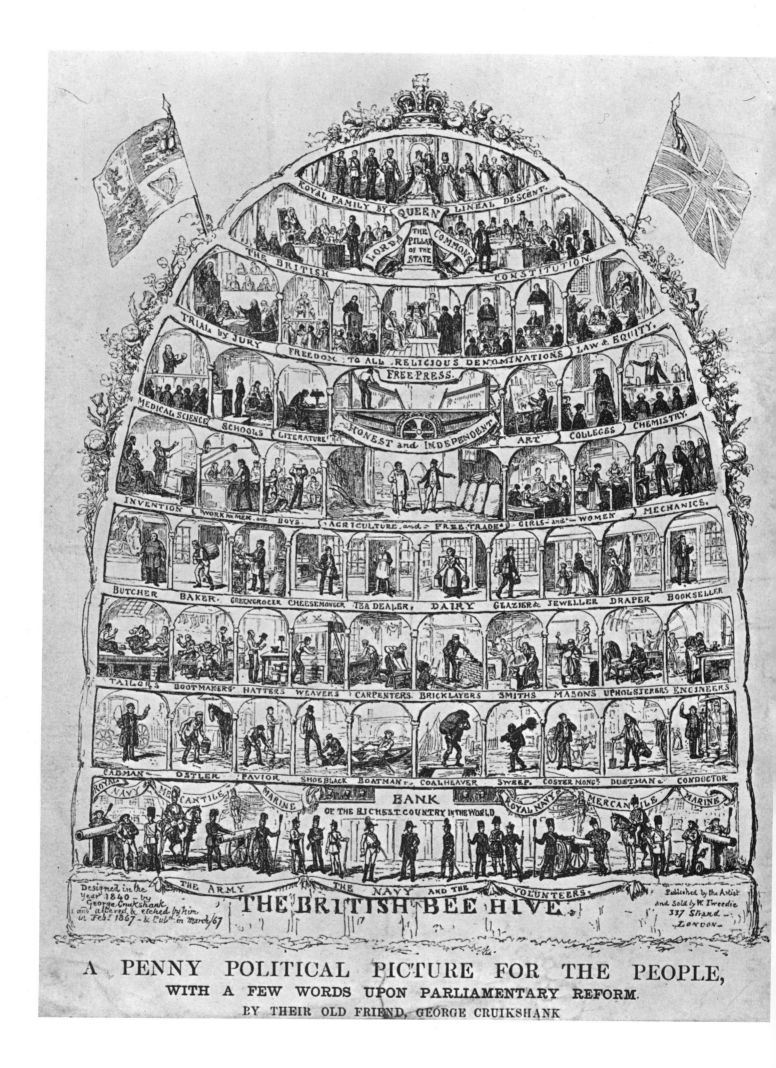

# ...to the Trades Union Congress of 1967

George Potter, militant editor of the labour journal "Beehive", and virtual leader of the London building trades, was one of the only two delegates from London to attend the first Trades Union Congress, 1868, in Manchester.

George Woodcock, T.U.C. general secretary since 1960, addressing the ninety-ninth Trades Union Congress at Brighton in September 1967.

"The British People's Beehive" (left). The cartoonist George Cruickshank's view of the stratified social structure of Britain, and of the gulfs between the governors and the governed, in 1867.

(Right) Some of the delegates to the 1967 Trades Union Congress, which by now was representative of some nine million trade union members; and which had become an active participant in the processes of planning the country's economy and social services.

*Robert Applegarth, secretary of the Amalgamated Carpenters, and the dominant figure in the Junta, the leadership of the London Trades Council.*

*William Allan, secretary of the Amalgamated Engineers. A man whose cautious nature and policies conditioned the Junta's reservations about George Potter's flamboyant militancy.*

*George Odger, an official of the Ladies Shoemakers, who, while still a working shoemaker himself, became the eloquent part-time secretary of the London Trades Council.*

# Members of the Junta and some of the political causes, at home and abroad, for which they rallied the support of trade unionists

"THE MINUTE-BOOKS of the London Trades Council from 1860 to 1867 present a mirror of the Trade Union history of this period . . .", wrote the Webbs. "In 1861–62, for instance, we see the Council trying vainly to settle the difficult problem of overlap between the trades of the shipwrights and the iron-shipbuilders . . .

"But the special interest of these minutes lies in their unconscious revelation of the way in which the Council become the instrument of the new policy of participation in general politics.

"Under Odger's influence, the Council took a prominent part in organising the popular welcome to Garibaldi, and in 1862 it held a great meeting in St. James's Hall in support of the struggle of the Northern States against negro slavery, at which John Bright was the principal speaker.

"In 1864, the Junta placed itself definitely in opposition to the 'Old Unionists', who objected to all connection between the Government and the concerns of working men."

# The international climate in which

*Confronted with the challenge of the Polish revolt against the Russians in 1863, the British government equivocated. But the Junta brought its people out on to the streets in unequivocal human solidarity with the Poles.*

## A GROWL FOR POLAND.

MR. BULL. "AH, OLD DOG—YOU'D LIKE TO HAVE ANOTHER RUN AT THAT BEAR, WOULDN'T YOU; BUT IT WON'T DO THIS TIME

**THE DERBY, 1867. DIZZY WINS WITH "REFORM BILL."**

*Garibaldi, architect of the Italian liberation campaign. When he came to London in 1864 members of the Junta were waiting to welcome him, and to organise demonstrations in his support.*

*Pressure by trade unionists at the 1865 general election, and the ensuing mass demonstrations of working people, gave Disraeli that basis of popular support which he needed in Parliament in order to secure the passage into law of the Reform Bill, whereby the working men in the towns were accorded the right to vote.*

## e TUC was born

*During the American Civil War, Abraham Lincoln and his men were fortified by fervent addresses of support sent to them by great meetings of British workers in Manchester and London, urging them to complete the task of abolishing slavery everywhere—not merely in the rebelling Southern States.*

M*R* R........ *PITY THE SORROWS OF A POOR OLD MAN.*

WORKMAN. *IT'S NO USE OLD BOY, WE'RE NOT TO BE CAUGHT WITH CHAFF, YOU'VE DECEIVED*
*IS THE MAN OF OUR CHOICE.*

*A contemporary cartoonist's view of the 1868 Parliamentary election in Sheffield, where, during the early 1860s, some crucial things had been happening. Now A. J. Mundella, a pro-trade union hosiery manufacturer, was adopted, with Sheffield Trades Council's backing, as Liberal candidate—thus displacing J. A. Roebuck, the anti-trade-union Liberal M.P. for Sheffield, who had been serving as a member of the Royal Commission of Inquiry into Trade Unions.*

# Some of the events which led up to the founding of the TUC: the Sheffield outrages . . . and the Royal Commission of Inquiry into Trade Unions

*J. A. Roebuck, from Sheffield. Of the eleven Royal Commissioners he was on of those most hostile to the unions.*

NEW FACTORY ACT 1868.
REGULATIONS.

ENOUGH, MUNDELLA

Nº 6

*Lord Elcho, appointed a member of the Royal Commission of Inquiry into Trade Unions, after serving, in 1866, as chairman of the Select Committee on the reform of the Master and Servant Law.*

*Sir William Erle, a former Chief Justice, who was appointed chairman of the Royal Commission, with instructions to "report on the organisation and rules of trades unions, and the several matters relating thereto".*

*Thomas Hughes, lawyer and Christian Socialist, who had been elected, with trade union support, as Radical M.P. for Lambeth. One of the Royal Commissioners most favourable to the unions.*

*Frederic Harrison, in later life. The Junta's nominee on the Royal Commission. "The unions have serious faults", he declared, "but I still believe them necessary as I do railways, and capable of improvement."*

THE CHAIN of cause and effect which led to the establishment of the Trades Union Congress can perhaps be most clearly traced in the course of events in Sheffield during the 1860s.

The dispute in the Sheffield file trades, which originated from a grinders' wage claim in September 1864, and came to a head with the grinders' strike of 1866, gradually revealed itself as a dispute which was basically not so much about wages as about the proposed introduction of new machinery for file-cutting, and the safeguards which the unions would deem necessary if they were to accept the new machines.

The Sheffield Trades Council (or Association of Organised Trades) realising that there was an important principle at stake, gave the file trade unions their full backing. The employers insisted on unconditional acceptance of machinery;

and the men struck. The A.O.T., hard pressed to find the necessary dispute pay, appealed for wider support. Both the Junta and George Potter's rival London Working Men's Association sent funds. And the Sheffield Trades Council adopted a suggestion of the Wolverhampton Trades Council, for a national conference of trades' delegates in Sheffield.

That conference, which assembled in July—some six weeks after the file trades strike had ended, virtually on the employers' terms—established a "permanent" (though short-lived) body, called the United Kingdom Alliance of Organised Trades. But, meantime, the repercussions of the "Sheffield outrages" —aggressive acts which had been perpetrated by a handful of militants against non-unionists and which culminated in the use of gunpowder to

blow up the house of one of them—had stimulated the outcry for an inquiry not only into these outrages, but into trade unions in general. Eventually the trade unions themselves, who were being increasingly accused in the newspapers of complicity in these outrages, felt obliged to ask for an inquiry in order to establish their innocence.

Accordingly, on November 17th a joint delegation from the Sheffield Trades Council and the London Trades Councils waited upon the Home Secretary with a request to that effect.

The special Commission to enquire specifically into the Sheffield outrages was not appointed until May 1867. But, significantly, the Government lost little time in setting up its Royal Commission of Inquiry into Trades Unions, which was appointed in February 1867.

George Howell, who became the first secretary of the T.U.C.'s Parliamentary Committee, which was set up by the 1871 Congress to lobby M.P.s for the amendment of the Criminal Law Amendment Bill.

Henry Broadhurst, the Stonemasons' leader who took over from Howell in 1875. He insisted at the 1877 Congress that the less they "interfered with the differences arising between trade and trade, and industry and industry, the better would it be . . ."

# First fruits of the TUC's efforts: the repeal of the Criminal Law Amendment Act

IN THE FULLNESS of time, the Royal Commission of Inquiry into Trade Unions was delivered of two Reports. The Majority Report proposed that certain steps should be taken to legalise the position of trade unions in certain limited respects. The Minority Report, signed by Hughes, Harrison and Lord Lichfield, simply recommended the complete legalisation of trade unions, and called for the total repeal of the restrictions of the 1825 Act.

In the event, the Government legislation which followed consisted of two contradictory measures. The Trade Union Act of 1871 legalised the status of trade unions and accorded protection to their funds. But the clauses on picketing and intimidation of the Criminal Law Amendment Act, which was part of the same year's package, left trade unionists as vulnerable to criminal prosecution as they had been before.

The Government of the day may have assumed that they had now made a final solution of the prickly trade union problem. But, as Henry Crompton pointed out in a document called

"Digest of Labour Laws", which he wrote with Frederic Harrison, and which was issued by the T.U.C.'s Parliamentary Committee in 1875, "the Judges declared that the only effect of the legislation of 1871 was to make the trade object of the strike not illegal. A strike was perfectly legal; but, if the means employed were calculated to coerce the employer, they were illegal means; and a combination to do a legal act by illegal means was a criminal conspiracy. In other words, a strike was lawful, but anything done in pursuance of a strike was criminal. Thus the judges tore up the remedial statute, and each fresh decision went further and developed new dangers."

So . . . the Trades Union Congress organised itself and the members it represented to remedy that "remedial statute". And the campaign which resulted, in 1875, in the Repeal of the Criminal Law Amendment Act proved to be by far the most important of the comparatively few effective operations which the T.U.C. was able to initiate in the whole period 1868–1900.

John Ruskin, whose book "Unto this Last" helped to jolt the public's preconceptions about the sanctity of classical political economy, and consequently about the valid role of trade unions in a country's economic life.

The 1867 Reform Act had given some working men the right to vote. But in casting their vote they still were obliged to choose between a Liberal and a Conservative candidate.

# Working men voting during the dinner hour

The King's Road, Chelsea scene in 1874.
Supporters of the Liberal candidates campaigning during the General Election.
George Howell and the Parliamentary Committee of the T.U.C. organised the putting of a series of "Test Questions" to Parliamentary candidates.

*How children were sent on their way to the coal face, cross-lapped upon the clatch-iron, in the golden reign of Queen Victoria.*

THREE COMMENTS made in that day and age go to the heart of the matter:

"You must just tell the Queen Victoria that we are guid loyal subjects; women people here don't mind work, but they object to horse-work; and that she would have the blessings of all the Scottish coal-women if she would get them out of the pits, and send them to other labour."

*Isabel Hogg, 53 years old, coal-bearer, quoted in report of 1842.*

And:

"Every man acquainted with the political history of the last half-century must know that the labour of children was actually pointed out to the manufacturers by Mr. William Pitt, as a new resource by which they might be enabled to bear the additional load of taxation which the necessities of the State compelled him to impose.

"The necessity for labour created by this taxation has not yet abated; because the immense capital taken away by the enormous expenditure of the great wars arising out of the French Revolution has not been replaced . . ."

*W. Cooke Taylor, Factories and the Factory System (1844).*

And:

"We find that instances occur in which children are taken into these mines to work as early as four years of age, sometimes at five, and between five and six, not infrequently between six and seven, and often from seven to eight, while from eight to nine is the ordinary age at which employment in these mines commences."

*—from the 1842 report of the Children's Employment Commission (Mines).*

which trade unionists set out to reform

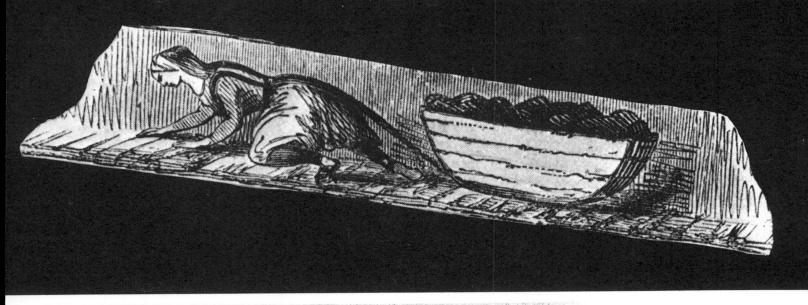

*Part of the labour force in a British cotton mill, around 1840.*

*Pay day for the children of the Industrial Revolution in booming Britain.*

As the Great Exhibition of 1851 displays to the world the fruits of Britain's manufacturing supremacy and proclaims the prosperity of her traders and industrialists, Punch confronts the conscience of the Victorian Establishment with the condition of some of the sweated workers, who, though they have contributed their life's work to that prosperity, are yet excluded from its benefits.

Mr Punch's heart may have been in the right place, but his use of words was a bit adrift. The "sweater" of those days was the exploiting employer, not the exploited employee.

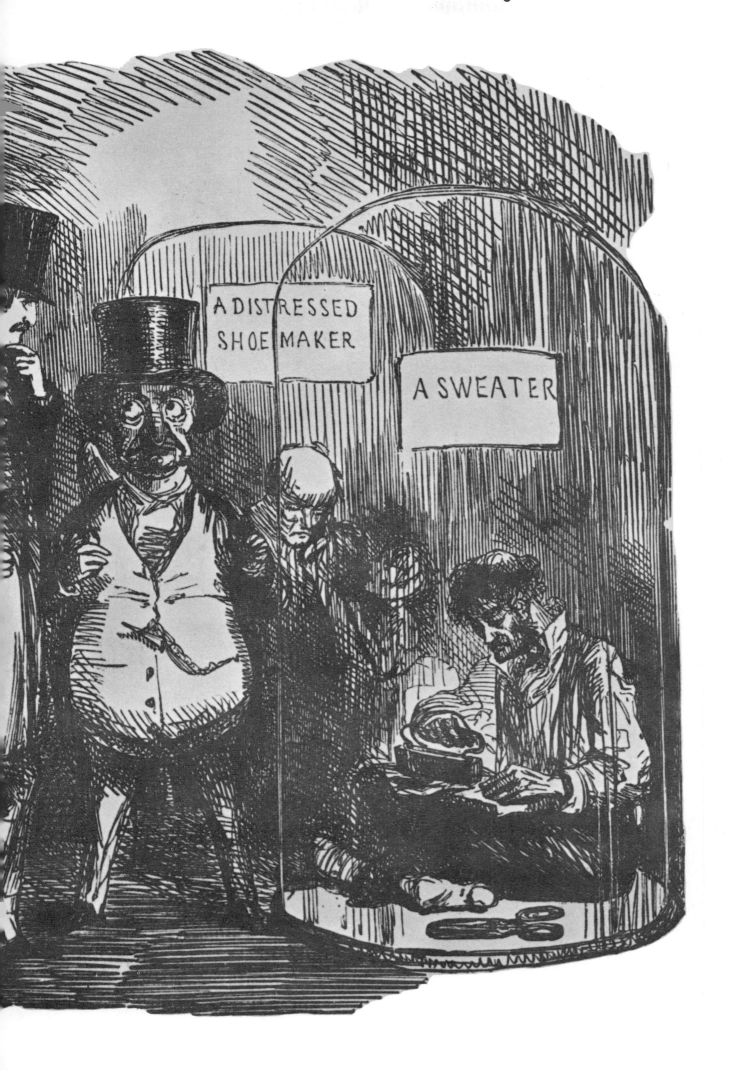

# The price of coal

*The toll of the 1870s. Disaster at Seaham: one of the rescue teams goes down.*

*Fire-fighting and (right) life-saving equipment of that day.*

*Disaster at the Troedyrhiw Colliery, 1877. Scene at the pithead.*

THE COAL MINES Regulation Act of 1860 had forbidden the employment of boys under twelve in the mines; but it had done nothing to solve the safety problem. A series of colliery disasters in the 1860s and a sustained agitation by the miners led to the passing, in 1872, of the Coal Mines Act, which decreed that every pit was to be tested for safety daily by deputy overseers, and also gave the miners the right to appoint some of their own people as inspectors.

But the disasters did not cease with the passing of the 1872 Act. In the trade slump of the 1870s, coal became cheap and so—with the resulting pressure to compensate for the low prices by increased output— did miners' lives.

In his book, "The Growth of British Industrial Relations", E. Phelps Brown describes the bitter fatalism of those days:

"The Welsh miner who was injured was carried home and laid on the kitchen table top for the doctor to operate on him there. The valley knew when a man was killed, for the whole shift came up, and walked behind his body till it was laid in his front room.

"Accidents might be accepted as part of life, but only because it was a hard life anyhow and there was no justice in it . . ."

*Disaster at the Haydock Colliery, 1878. Following explosion, some two hundred lives were lost. The ma the centre is Mr. John Turton, manager of the pit, described as "the first rescu*

Some of the consequences of the lack of safety regulations which the Coal Mines Act of 1872 was designed to remedy

# The moving spirit behind the miners' unions— who believed that 'A man's a man, for a' that!'

*Alexander McDonald, Scottish miners' leader.*

IN 1856, Alexander McDonald came south from Scotland to England, as the envoy of the Scottish Miners' Association; and, travelling from lodge to lodge, he in due course brought into being the National Miners' Association—a loose-knit body into which he infused his own fervent belief in the efficacy of bringing pressure upon governments as a means of getting things done.

Thus McDonald, and the conferences which he organised, played a decisive part in the campaign for the Coal Mines Act of 1872—as he had already done in the Glasgow Trades Council's campaign for the repeal of the Master and Servant Law in 1867.

G. D. H. Cole wrote of him: "The craftsmen who laid down regulations for the conduct of their trade were affirming the dignity of their calling, as well as seeking to get a good price for their labour-power. To regard their rules simply as so many restrictions on the employer's right to turn their labour to such uses as he might please was to assume that the labourer could properly be treated as no more than an instrument of production, devoid of human claims."

Two of the 19th century's 'instruments of production'

The "Flying Dutchman" comes to grief on the Great Western Railway, 1876. It was in order to bring pressure on the Government to restrict railwaymen's long working hours, and thus incidentally to reduce the toll of accidents, that the Amalgamated Society of Railway Servants had been founded, with the help of middle-class patrons, in 1871.

# The campaigns to obtain proper compensation for industrial injuries . . . and adequate safeguards for seamen

Michael Bass, brewer, millionaire and Liberal M.P. for Derby, who helped bring this first railwaymen's union into being.

THE 1880 Employers Liability Act, which was of particular concern to miners and railwaymen, only went part of the way advocated by the T.U.C. It gave the worker a general legal claim for damages arising out of injury or accident at work; but the employer was still able to evade responsibility if the injury was caused by a worker "in common employment" with the victim. Only much later, in 1897, did the Government completely accept that compensation of the victim or his dependants for industrial accident or injury must be met by industry, no matter how the accident had been caused. Even then, seamen were excluded from this protection.

Meanwhile, during the 1870s, the seamen gained some benefit from the Merchant Shipping Act of 1876, sponsored by Samuel Plimsoll, whose "Plimsoll Line" was designed to protect them from the hazards of over-loaded vessels. But, though copies of Plimsoll's book, "Our Seamen", were passed round the Trades Union Congress of 1873, little was done to create a national seamen's union until 1887 when the National Amalgamated Sailors and Firemen's Union was formed.

*A "coffin ship" of the early 1870s, in port. One of those overcrowded, insanitary and often unseaworthy vessels which were a menace to seamen, and to which Samuel Plimsoll turned his ardent attention.*

*Samuel Plimsoll, Liberal M.P., addressing the House of Commons in his crusade for safety at sea.*

*Joseph Arch, the inspired Warwickshire farm labourer who, in 1872, established the National Agricultural Labourers' Union, which enrolled 100,000 members by the end of the following year.*

*Arch's union and its activities infuriated the squires, who raged "with indescribable bitterness" against these "meetings of rural labourers —meetings positively where men made speeches".*

"... TO ELEVATE the social position of the farm labourers of the county by assisting them to increase their wages;
"to lessen the number of ordinary working hours;
"to improve their habitations;
"to provide them with gardens or allotments;
"and to assist deserving and suitable labourers to migrate and emigrate."

Such were some of the declared objects of the Warwickshire Agricultural Labourers' Union, the immediate forerunner of the National Agricultural Labourers' Union—both of which were founded in 1872 by the farm labourer and Primitive Methodist lay preacher, Joseph Arch.

On the wages front, Arch's union, working towards the same ends as the Lincolnshire Labour League and the Kent and Sussex Labourers' Union, made spectacular but short-lived advances. In 1870, the average weekly wage of a farm labourer had stood at 12/- a week, a rise of 2/6 on the 1850 level. By 1875, after three years of union pressure, the average wage had risen to some 55 per cent above the 1850 level.

Then, farm-produce prices slumped. Farmers became ruthless in the use of the lock-out. Wage-levels fell back. And, in spite of the support of trade unionists like Odger and Potter, and Radicals like Herbert and Dilke, and eminent churchmen like Manning and Girdlestone, the influence of Arch's union was gradually but decisively broken.

*The Roman Catholic Cardinal Manning (above) and the Church of England Canon Girdlestone both came out staunchly in favour of Arch's union.*

32

# The struggle of the farm labourers' unions drew the support of the urban unions—but sharply divided the churchmen

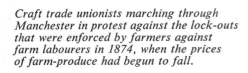

Craft trade unionists marching through Manchester in protest against the lock-outs that were enforced by farmers against farm labourers in 1874, when the prices of farm-produce had begun to fall.

Dr. Ellicot, Bishop of Gloucester, came out with the un-Christian recommendation that agricultural union agitators should be thrown into the village horse-ponds. Most country parsons also fell in behind the squirearchy.

*"A London School-Board capture, 2.40 a.m.", says the caption to this contemporary drawing of school-children being rounded up in 1871—one year after the passing of the Forster Education Act, introducing State education.*

# The advent of State education . . .

WITH THE Education Act of 1870, the State tentatively began the process of assuming responsibility for the elementary education of children of parents who could not afford to pay for it. It provided for the setting up of School Boards, elected by ratepayers, in districts where the local children were not adequately catered for by the voluntary schools there available. The School Boards were required to create enough Board schools to fill the gaps.

Many Churchmen revolted at the idea of Board Schools and the undenominational education which went with them. But a Board School was reckoned by the mass of poorer parents to be a great deal better than no school. Later, by an Act of 1876, education was made legally compulsory for children up to the age of twelve; and in 1898 Congress passed a resolution in favour of equality of opportunity in education. This demanded: the provision of school meals; the abolition of the half-time system; the raising of the school age to fifteen; the improved training of teachers; and

*Pupils in a Seven Dials Board School, in 1885. Six years later, State education was made free.*

*The Spartan aspect of the Mount Charles Elementary School at St. Austell, Cornwall. This was the first School Board school to be built under the provisions of the 1870 Education Act. It had room for 375 children. And it cost £940 to build. The building has changed little since those days. And it is still in use as a school.*

# ...and the birth of white-collar unions

the meeting by the National Exchequer of the costs of educating the nation's children.

That was just half a century after the following prescient exhortation had appeared in the Flint Glass Makers' Magazine: "If you do not wish to stand as you are and suffer more oppression, we say to you get knowledge, and in getting knowledge you get power . . . Let us earnestly advise you to educate; get intelligence instead of alcohol—it is sweeter and more lasting."

About this time there sprang up, alongside the now well-established and powerful craft unions a number of small but nevertheless vigorous trade unions of non-manual workers. The National Union of Elementary Teachers for instance, had been founded in 1860. Even within the Victorian Civil Service, the Post Office telegraphists managed to set up an Association of their own in 1881; and the provincial Post Office clerks followed suit in 1886. Thirteen years later railway clerks took the same step.

*Members of the Shop Assistants Union, who were to affiliate to the T.U.C. in 1899.*

*"Bloody Sunday", November 13th, 1887. As the police set about the unemployed demonstrators in Trafalgar Square, Mr. R. H. B. Marsham, the Magistrate of Greenwich Police Court, arrives on the scene with an escort of Her Majesty's Life Guards.*

# The trade union leaders of the unemployed and some of their political allies

*Left to right, Tom Mann and John Burns, both of the Amalgamated Society of Engineers, and both members of the Social Democratic Federation; and Will Thorne, the gasworker and member of the S.D.F. who organised the gasworkers' union and became a leading campaigner for the eight-hour day.*

*Another sector of the "Bloody Sunday" battlefield: St. Martin's Lane, where the police attempted to head off a contingent of unemployed men from the Clerkenwell Green area.*

*The morning after one of the many turbulent demonstrations of 1886: trade union and socialist leaders—including H. M. Hyndman, second from left, and John Burns, fourth from left—appear at Bow Street Police Court.*

*Left to right, Mrs. Annie Besant, Fabian and free thinker, whose writing inspired the successful matchgirls' strike of 1888; H. H. Champion, polemical journalist and former regular army officer, who helped organise and drill the unemployed marchers; and H. M. Hyndman, former City man who, under the influence of Marx's works, founded the Social Democratic Federation.*

*Charles Booth*

## Abroad: the first links with American trade unions are forged

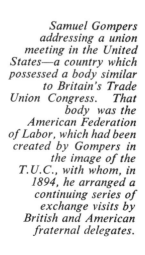

*Samuel Gompers addressing a union meeting in the United States—a country which possessed a body similar to Britain's Trade Union Congress. That body was the American Federation of Labor, which had been created by Gompers in the image of the T.U.C., with whom, in 1894, he arranged a continuing series of exchange visits by British and American fraternal delegates.*

*"Charles Booth's investigation into 'Life and Labour in London' (begun in order to refute S.D.F. propaganda)" wrote G. D. H. Cole and Raymond Postgate, "and the great dock strike of 1889 showed up enormous stagnant pools of misery and degradation which society and the Trade Union leaders had both forgotten. When Robert Lowe, as Chancellor of the Exchequer, proposed a tax upon matches which would have thrown a number of East End women out of work, Westminster was invaded by a 'deputation' of filthy and haggard harridans whom the London which saw them for the first time considered to be only half human. . . ."*

*Two of the great social investigators of the day, and co-authors of the first classic book on British Trade Unions: Sidney Webb and his wife Beatrice, who was one of Charles Booth's researchers and collaborators on his great survey, "Life and Labour in London".*

# The TUC on the brink of a new century

KEIR HARDIE, passionate advocate of a truly independent Labour Party, was always a rather unwelcome figure at the Trades Union Congress, which he ruthlessly and persistently attacked as having tepid policies and flaccid leadership.

There was, in fact, plenty to criticise. In the first thirty years or so after its foundation, the T.U.C., as such, could chalk up no more than two major achievements to its credit: the Repeal of the Criminal Law Amendment Act, already mentioned; and the introduction of the Fair Wages Clause.

The latter originated in a resolution passed by the 1888 Congress. It demanded, successfully, that a principle already practised by H.M. Stationery Office, which was by now allocating printing contracts only to firms observing trade union standards and conditions, should be extended to other Government departments and to local authorities.

On the debit side, the T.U.C. had, in the eyes of its critics then and later, let a number of crucial issues go by default. According to G. D. H. Cole, for example, the Parliamentary Committee's policy of non-intervention in demarcation disputes between one union and another was continued right through to the end of the century; by which time, demarcation disputes were causing havoc among the shipbuilding and engineering trade unions.

Then, in the last five years of the century, two things happened which further aroused the anger of the critics. In 1895, the T.U.C. excluded from Congress the local trades councils who had hitherto always been represented there as of right; because, said the T.U.C. leadership, such representation resulted in duplicated membership. But some sceptics believed that the leadership felt that the trades councils were an awkwardly militant element.

Next, the Conciliation Act, which empowered the Board of Trade to appoint, on request, conciliators and arbitrators in industrial disputes, passed into law. The intervention of Government as a conciliator in trade disputes was a significant development in industrial relations to which Congress paid not the slightest attention.

All the same, the fact that unions were still prepared to pay affiliation fees to the T.U.C. suggests that Congress had a useful role in bringing the representatives of unions together once a year—and in drawing the attention of Governments and society to the social and economic needs of workers and their families. From this, at least, a vital sense of movement was already developing.

*James Keir Hardie, the Ayrshire miners' leader, who was destined to become the first leader of the Labour Party.*

# A portent of the 'New Unionism': the matchgirls' strike of 1888

*Some of the few hundred match workers at Bryant and May's who struck, and won their case, and proceeded to organise their own union. In the same year, a resolution was moved in Congress by Miss Black of London: "That in the opinion of this Congress it is desirable, in the interests of both men and women, that in trades where women do the same work as men, they shall receive the same payment."*

# SOUTH SIDE
# CENTRAL STRIKE COMMITTEE,
## SAYES COURT, DEPTFORD.

SEPTEMBER 10, 1889.

# GENERAL MANIFESTO.

Owing to the fact that the demands of the Corn Porters, Deal Porters, Granary Men, General Steam Navigation Men, Permanent Men and General Labourers on the South Side have been misrepresented, the above Committee have decided to issue this Manifesto, stating the demands of the various sections now on Strike, and pledge themselves to support each section in obtaining their demands.

**DEAL PORTERS** of the Surrey Commercial Docks have already placed their demands before the Directors.

**LUMPERS (Outside)** demand the following Rates, viz:—1. 10d. per standard for Deals. 2. 11d. per stand. for all Goods rating from 2 x 4 to 2½ x 7, or for rough boards. 3. 1s. per std. for plain boards. Working day from 7 a.m. to 5 p.m., and that no man leave the "Red Lion" corner before 6.45 a.m. Overtime at the rate of 6d. per hour extra from 5 p.m. including meal times.

**STEVEDORES (Inside)** demand 8d. per hour from 7 a.m. to 5 p.m. 1s. per hour overtime. Overtime to commence from 5 p.m. to 7 a.m. Pay to commence from leaving "Red Lion" corner. Meal times to be paid for. Holidays & Meal times double pay, and that the Rules of the United Stevedores Protection League be acceded to in every particular. *conceded*

**OVERSIDE CORN PORTERS (S.C.D.)** demand 15s.3d. per 100 qrs. for Oats. Heavy labour 17s.4d. per 100 qrs. manual, or with use of Steam 16s.1d. All overtime after 6 p.m. to be paid at the rate of ½d. per qr. extra.

**QUAY CORN PORTERS** (S.C.D.) demand the return of Standard prices previous to March 1889, which had been in operation for 17 years.

**TRIMMERS AND GENERAL LABOURERS** demand 6d. per hour from 7 a.m. to 6 p.m. and 8d. per hour Overtime. Meal times as usual; and not to be taken on for less than 4 hours.

**WEIGHERS & WAREHOUSEMEN** demand to be reinstated in their former positions without distinction.

**BERMONDSEY AND ROTHERHITHE WALL CORN PORTERS** demand: 1. Permanent Men 30s. per week. 2. Casual Men 5s. 10d. per day and 8d. per hour Overtime; Overtime to commence at 6 p.m. Meal times as usual.

**GENERAL STEAM NAVIGATION MEN** demand:—1. Wharf Men, 6d. per hour from 6 a.m. to 6 p.m. and 8d. per hour Overtime. 2. In the Stream, 7d. per hour ordinary time, 9d. per hour Overtime. 3. In the Dock, 8d. per hour ordinary time, 1s. per hour Overtime.

**MAUDSLEY'S ENGINEER'S MEN.** Those receiving 21s. per week now demand 24s., and those receiving 24s. per week demand 26s.

**ASHBY'S, LTD., CEMENT WORKS** demand 6d. per ton landing Coals and Chalk. General Labourers 10% rise of wages all round, this making up for a reduction made 3 years ago.

**GENERAL LABOURERS,** TELEGRAPH CONSTRUCTION demand 4s. per day from 6 a.m. to 5 p.m., time and a quarter for first 2 hours Overtime, and if later, time and a half for all Overtime. No work to be done in Meal Hours.

Signed on behalf of the Central Committee, Wade Arms,

BEN. TILLETT,
JOHN BURNS,
TOM MANN,
H. H. CHAMPION,
JAS. TOOMEY.

Signed on behalf of the South side Committee,

JAS. SULLI
CHAS. H
HUGH J

side to be sent to Mr. HUGH BRO

Central Strike Committee, Sayes Court,

*The Strike Committee's manifesto, issued in the fourth week of the strike. In a few days—on September 16th—the striking dockers, after winning practically everything they had demanded, went triumphantly back to work. And forthwith started forming the Dock, Wharf, Riverside and General Labourers Union.*

# The great dockers' strike of 1889

*One of the great marches through the City of London that were organised by John Burns to compel the nation to give its reluctant attention to the dockers' two principal claims: the claim for the abolition of contract work, a chief cause of sweated labour, and the claim for a minimum wage of sixpence an hour—the "dockers' tanner".*

IT ALL BEGAN with a strike of a few labourers at the West India Dock, on August 13th, 1889, only a few days after the London gas-workers, led by Will Thorne, had confronted the gas companies with the demand for an eight-hour day —and got it. Ben Tillett, secretary of the "Tea Workers' and General Labourers Union", and the strikers' spokesman, received immediate offers of help from those two tireless militants, John Burns and Tom Mann. The strike spread to the East India Dock, and the Port of London was brought to a standstill.

The dockers' marches through the City, stage-managed by Burns and made spectacular by the banners and emblems and totem poles crowned with stinking fish-heads and rotting onions—current samples of the dockers' diet—went from strength to strength; but the strikers' relief funds sank lower and lower. Until, finally, the desperate choice facing the strikers seemed to be between capitulation and the forlorn hope of calling a strike of all trades in London.

Then suddenly, out of the blue from Australia, money began to pour in for the sustenance of the London strikers. Money from the wharf labourers of Brisbane; from almost every Australian trade union; from Australian football clubs. About £30,000 in all: a sum to make the dock companies jittery, and reluctantly disposed to meet with a mediation committee that was set up in the Mansion House by the Lord Mayor (who subsequently withdrew) but which was endowed with the persistent assistance of that remarkable conciliator Cardinal Manning.

The dockers obtained the major part of what they wanted. A famous victory, which lifted the hearts not only of the London dockers, but of other workers—gas-workers, rail-waymen, textile workers, building workers, shipbuilding and metal workers, miners and boot and shoe operatives, all of whom drew their own moral from the story of the struggle for the dockers' tanner, and rallied to their own appropriate unions.

One of the emblems carried in the strikers' processions through London. The docker's diminutive child. This was contrasted with the employer's robust child. The docker's dinner was contrasted with the employer's dinner; the docker's cat with the employer's cat.

Ben Tillett, who, when the strike began, was the secretary of a small tea warehousemen's society, and who, soon after it ended, became the full-time secretary of the new and immediately powerful Dock, Wharf, Riverside and General Labourers Union.

# The strikers win 'the full round orb of the docker's tanner'—and the prestige of the new unionists soars

Ben Tillett (in the left foreground) and Cardinal Manning (at the far corner of the table, right) at a meeting of the ad hoc mediation committee at the Mansion House, with John Burns (in the right foreground). Mainly from the efforts of these three men and of thousands of anonymous dockers, the satisfactory settlement of the great docks strike emerged.

*A food convoy guarded by troops in armoured cars moves through the City of London during the 1926 General Strike at the end of a period marked by bitter industrial unrest yet not without several indications of better things to come. For the first time the TUC was brought into close consultation with the Government over several important measures and a system of industrial relations based on national negotiations for each industry was recommended by the Whitley Committee.*

WE REQUIRE 8 HOURS FOR WORK · 8 HOURS FOR OUR OWN INSTRUCTION AND 8 HOURS FOR REPOSE

# 1900-1928: The TUC is consulted by Ministers and begins to take part in public administration

THE SECOND PHASE in the development of the Trades Union Congress really begins with the crippling House of Lords Taff Vale decision in 1901 and ends with the General Strike in 1926.

During the early years of the century the TUC was still anxious to influence the Government with a view to protecting trade unions and the individual worker. The most important success at that time was the passing into law of the Trade Disputes Bill—"the main Charter of Trade Unionism". In the following years, the T.U.C. began to be called into consultation by Cabinet Ministers about projected government legislation. The T.U.C. was consulted by Winston Churchill about the establishment of a system of Labour Exchanges, and by Lloyd George about his scheme for social insurance. And the T.U.C. was not only consulted; it was also invited to participate in the administration of government by nominating men to help operate both these schemes.

But alongside these developments in the T.U.C.'s functions there also developed in the trade union Movement, during the middle years of this period, the growth of the challenging syndicalist idea that it could be the destined eventual role of trade unions (and of the T.U.C. or some alternative leadership) to take over and embody in themselves the key political powers of government. The success of national strikes before the First World War, and the rise of the shop stewards' movement during it, seemed at first to lend some substance to this shadowy vision of ultimate workers' control of both industry and the State.

Back in 1901, however, the urgent need for legislation to reverse the Taff Vale Judgement and its brutal threat to trade union funds seemed to many trade unionists to demand above all the immediate formation and support of an independent political party, representing the interests of the whole working class movement, whose elected Members of Parliament would spur on the House of Commons to pass this crucial piece of legislation.

Such a party had been advocated by Keir Hardie on his first appearance at a Trades Union Congress, in 1887. Six years later, the project had received a resounding boost from Sidney Webb and Bernard Shaw who, in an historic article, "To your tents, O Israel", argued that trade unionists would never get things done through the Liberal Members of Parliament whom they were at this time supporting, since the Liberal Government had proved itself unwilling to meet the fair claims and grievances even of its own employees.

But it took the menacing potentialities of the Taff Vale Judgement to persuade the trade unions to accord to this idea, and to its current incarnation, the "Labour Representation Committee", some measure of active support.

In fact, the L.R.C. had itself stemmed from the persistently frustrating Parliamentary situation, which had been described thus to the 1899 Congress by the Parliamentary Committee:—"Your Committee again wish to point out that with the present mode of procedure of the House of Commons it is almost impossible to get any useful Bill through the House, unless the Government allow it to pass by withdrawing its opposition; and, in their opinion, if any remedy is to be effected, it must be done by the working class at the polls".

At the 1906 general election, the working classes at the polls gave the House of Commons a refreshingly new look. And the 29 Labour Representation Committee M.P.s, together with Members sponsored by the Parliamentary Committee, were able to apply enough pressure to induce the Liberal Government to base its Trade Disputes Bill on the principles which the Parliamentary Committee of the T.U.C. had itself laid down, for the purpose of reversing the situation arising out of the Taff Vale Judgement.

Even during the difficult last months of the previous Conservative government the Parliamentary Committee had promoted—and intensively lobbied M.P.s for—a whole series of "useful Bills", dealing with such things as workmen's compensation, traffic regulations, compulsory weighing where workers were paid by the ton, and "textile workers" weekend holidays. But the Trades Dispute Act of 1906 was the Parliamentary Committee's culminating achievement at this time.

The drafting and promotion of these Bills involved a great deal of work for the Parliamentary Committee's legal adviser, Mr. Edmond Browne, who had been appointed in 1900; and particularly for the Secretary of the T.U.C. and his one clerk. So much so that, in 1904, when Sam Woods of the Miners' Federation (who had been elected Secretary of the T.U.C. annually in each of the previous 10 years) was forced to resign through ill-health and was succeeded by W. C. Steadman of the Barge Builders' Union, Congress at last took the view that the post of Secretary should be both a permanent and a full-time one.

With this re-inforced support behind them, the L.R.C. M.P.s and those sponsored by the Parliamentary Committee, now all known as "The Labour Party" were able between 1906 and 1911 to press the Liberal Government to pass several Acts dealing with subjects which had been consistently canvassed by the T.U.C.—such as the limitation of underground work in coal mines, the establishment of labour exchanges, the fixing of legal minimum wages in sweated industries (which employed a very high proportion of women workers) and old age pensions.

But the fact that these Acts seldom dealt really adequately with the problems concerned caused many of the more militant trade unionists to grow increasingly cynical about the efficacy of parliamentary action, and, indeed, about the usefulness of political parties. It was thus that, in 1910, the syndicalist Tom Mann, and visiting American emissaries of the Industrial Workers of the World, and British Guild Socialists were able to obtain an eager, though limited, hearing for their passionate views on industrial unionism, or on National Guilds; and for their visions or fantasies of workers' control—control, first, of industry, and ultimately of the whole State machinery of government.

"Pure" Syndicalism was the subject of serious debate inside the trade union Movement—and chiefly in the mining and transport industries—for scarcely more than three years. But the rise of the shop stewards during the First World War gave the general cause of industrial unionism a considerable lift. The Webbs have recorded "the rapid adoption between 1913 and 1920 by many of the younger leaders of the movement . . . and, subject to various modifications, also by some of the most powerful Trade Unions, of this new ideal of the development of the existing Trade • Unions into self-organised, self-contained, self-governing industrial democracies, as supplying the future method of conducting industries and services. The schemes put forward by the N.U.R., the Miners Federation and the Union of Postal Workers differ widely from the revolutionary Syndicalism of Mr. Tom Mann and the large visions of the Industrial Workers of the World. . . . In fact, they limit the claim of the manual workers merely to participation in the management, fully conceding that the final authority must be vested in the community of citizens or consumers".

In fact, the syndicalist's aspects of industrial unionism were destined never to become a dominant factor in the British movement.

The attitude adopted to this question by the majority of trade unionists was probably best expressed by Harry Gosling of the Lightermen's Union, in his presidential address to the 1916 Congress, in which he also forecast the need for greatly increased responsibilities, facilities and powers for the Parliamentary Committee, or some equivalent body, in order to match the growing strength of the organised employers' associations.

"We do not seek", said Gosling, "to sit on the board of directors, or to interfere with the buying of materials, or with the selling of the product. But in daily management of the employment in which we spend our working lives, in the atmosphere and under the conditions in which we have to work, in the hours of beginning and ending work, in the conditions of remuneration, and even in the manner and practices of the foreman with whom we have to be in contact, in all these matters we feel that we, as workmen, have a right to a voice —even to an equal voice—with the management itself".

In December, 1919, the Parliamentary Committee of the T.U.C., having followed up the main refrain of Gosling's speech, reported to Congress the need "for the development of more adequate machinery for the co-ordination of Labour activities, both for the movement as a whole, and especially for its industrial side".

So, in 1920, thanks largely to the continuing dedicated efforts of Harry Gosling, who was warmly supported by Ernest Bevin, the General Council of the T.U.C. was brought to birth.

One of the first problems they faced was falling trade union membership. The massive wartime growth could not be sustained in the face of mounting unemployment—and given the consequent popular feeling in favour of co-ordination policies, the General Council were able to encourage several important amalgamations between different unions within a single industry. In the first half of the 1920s—before, during and after the short-lived first Labour Government—the T.U.C. improved its headquarters organisation by setting up a number of different departments; and in 1925 it for the first time entered the main educational area.

One fundamental issue in public education policy between the two world wars was the extension of secondary education, towards which both governments and local authorities tried fitfully to move. Most politicians and public servants thought of education chiefly as an area in which economies in public spending could, when desirable, be suitably made.

The T.U.C. strenuously resisted what it called "these false economies" and kept pressing for general educational reform. In 1925, the T.U.C. for the first time gave evidence to the Consultative Committee of the Board of Education, about the education of adolescents. Later, that Committee, in its most distinguished report—the first Hadow Report—endorsed the T.U.C.'s view that all children should have secondary education in purpose-built secondary schools.

So the General Council's responsibilities and field of activities had become very wide; but the powers which they had been accorded by the unions in Congress were still limited. Some of those limitations were exposed in the course of the "General", or national, Strike of 1926, in which the T.U.C.'s powers to "co-ordinate industrial action", including action for the settlement of disputes, were shown to be still incomplete.

At that time, when the miners themselves had failed to make any headway towards the settlement of their claims, a Conference of Trade Union Executives was called by the General Council, to consider co-ordinated action in support of the miners, and to give the T.U.C. authority to handle the conduct of the dispute. Mr. Herbert Smith, for the Miners, said they understood the position was that all negotiations would now be carried on through the General Council but that they, as the Miners' Federation, would be consulted.

The General Council came within an ace of negotiating a fair settlement; but when printers at the Daily Mail refused to print the paper because of a leading article hostile to the strike, the Conservative Government—whose brutally deflationist back-to-the-Gold-Standard policy had led up to the situation— seized the opportunity to break off negotiations with the General Council.

The National Strike began; and, as it proceeded, it became clear that the question of who was entitled to agree a settlement on behalf of the striking unions had not been explicitly decided in advance. The General Council and the Miners' Federation each claimed that they themselves were the only people so entitled.

Both sides stuck to their guns, which by now were pointing in quite different directions. And so, in this disastrously unco-ordinated situation, the General Council called off the General Strike, on Wednesday May 12 and the miners were left to go it alone. ∎

# In the wake of the 1906 general election the Parliamentary Labour Party is born

*Some of the 54 Labour and Lib.-Lab. M.P.s who arrived at Westminster after the electoral rout of the Conservatives. Of these 54, nine were members of the Parliamentary Committee of the T.U.C., and no fewer than 29 were sponsored by the Labour Representation Committee, which now proceeded to change its name to the Labour Party.*

"The general election of 1906" wrote E. Phelps Brown, "is a landmark in our social history. . . ." It was not simply the swing of a familiar pendulum, but marked the opening of a new era. It had been brought in by general elementary education, votes for wage-earners, and a heightened resentment against the industrial system."

# The TUC's own charter of trade unionism is passed into law

THE LABOUR Representation Committee, in which I.L.P. politicians and socialists were active from the beginning, at first received only fitful and tepid support from trade unionists and the T.U.C. Then, in 1901, came the House of Lords decision upholding the Taff Vale Judgement, which ruled that a trade union could be sued and compelled to pay for damages inflicted by its officials.

It now became clear to the T.U.C. and the Parliamentary Committee that, if the right to strike was ever to be preserved as an essential instrument of trade union policy, then the new principle embodied in the Taff Vale decision must be reversed by Parliament. If this was to be done, the trade unions must secure greater and more influential representation in Parliament.

If the T.U.C.'s Parliamentary Committee was incapable of achieving this on its own, then a, working arrangement must be sought with the Labour Representation Committee— politicians, socialists and all—for the joint, or complementary, endorsement of Parliamentary candidates.

In the event, at the 1906 general election, the working arrangements worked like a charm. Fifty-four "Labour" candidates, of various sorts, were returned; in some cases greatly to their own surprise. And, in the same year, the new Liberal Government under Sir Harry Campbell-Bannerman, finding that a very large number of Liberal M.P.'s had pledged themselves during the election campaign to support the T.U.C. Parliamentary Committee's own Trade Disputes Bill, felt obliged to accept the principles of the T.U.C.'s Bill and pass them into law. And the Lords deemed it wiser not to obstruct the Bill's passage. Thus was restored to trade unions the degree of legal immunity which had been theirs before the Taff Vale Judgement. And, as Henry Pelling put it, "the unions had secured from the ballot box the respect for their privileged position which had been denied them in the courts."

The next alarm on the legal front was destined to arise out of yet another House of Lords decision, upholding the Court of Appeal's Osborne Judgement of 1909, which ruled that it was unlawful for trade unions to contribute to political funds.

*David Lloyd-George, with his wife and daughter Megan. In 1908, he had become Chancellor of the Exchequer in Asquith's Government of which the once militant trade unionist and socialist John Burns was also a member, as President of the Local Government Board. It was Lloyd George rather than Burns, who piloted through the Liberal Government's Old Age Pensions Act, a rather mean and watered-down version of the kind of Pensions Bill for which the T.U.C. had long been lobbying.*

*The Act, which came into force on January 1st 1909, applied to people "who are 70 years of age, and whose income does not exceed £31 10 0 per annum. The amount of the pension varies from 5/- a week for persons with incomes not exceeding £21, down to 1/- a week".*

*Opinion inside the Labour Movement was sharply divided about the desirability of the National Insurance Bill. The Parliamentary Committee of the T.U.C. on the whole approved it. But trade unionists were divided about it, and many socialists deplored the contributory basis of the scheme which, they insisted, ought to be financed by taxation.*
*In April, 1911, the T.U.C. formed, together with representatives of the General Federation of Trade Unions, a sub-committee to nominate men for the provisional insurance committees. This was another early instance of the T.U.C. moving into the field of participation in the administration of government.*

*Winston Churchill, as President of the Board of Trade in Asquith's Government, was responsible for steering through the Commons a Bill to establish Labour Exchanges. Before and during the passage of the Bill, Churchill constantly consulted the Parliamentary Committee of the T.U.C. This was a first portent of the kind of direct relationship between T.U.C. and Government that was to develop during and after the First World War. In fact, the T.U.C. had already done considerable research on their own account in this field: the Parliamentary Committee had sent a delegation to Germany to examine their*

*Labour Exchange system and the compulsory insurance scheme for sickness and unemployment.*
*When the Labour Exchange system was set up here, Churchill chose D. J. Shackleton, then President of the Trades Union Congress, as trade union member of the three-man committee whose task was to appoint the most important officials who would be operating it. Another portent: this time of the increasing part which the T.U.C. was destined to play, at the invitation of future governments, in social administration.*

# Under TUC pressure two Liberal leaders start to lay the foundations of a welfare state

*A contemporary artist's impression of one of Britain's first labour exchanges, which had been demanded by the T.U.C. for several years.*

DURING the first four years of Asquith's Administration which was formed in the summer of 1908, the T.U.C., operating chiefly through its Parliamentary Committee, continued its original policy of attempting to influence the government of the day with a view to introducing legislation for the increased protection and benefit of trade unions and of individual working men and women. And, during those years, Congress pressures met with considerable success, as the records show:—

In 1908, the Mines Regulation Act, which limited the hours of underground work to eight a day, was finally passed by a rather reluctant Liberal Government; and, in the following year, the miners' representatives in the Commons, who had hitherto sat as Lib-Labs but were now disillusioned by Liberal hesitations, transferred their allegiance to the Labour Party.

In 1909, Winston Churchill introduced his Trades Boards Bill, which established trade boards with powers to fix minimum wages in certain notoriously sweated industries employing a majority of women workers—ready-made tailoring, cardboard box-making, ready-made blouse making and machine-made lace and net finishing. In the case of this particular Bill, popular support was mobilised not so much by the T.U.C. and its Parliamentary Committee (who were deeply preoccupied with pushing the Right to Work Bill) as by the Women's Trade Union League, whose dedicated leaders were Mary Macarthur and Susan Lawrence.

In the same year, however, there passed on to the Statute Book two Bills which did owe a great deal to T.U.C. advocacy and research:—the Old Age Pensions Bill and the Bill to establish Labour Exchanges.

It is true that most of these measures became law in a form less satisfactory than that which the T.U.C. had visualised and advocated. But these measures did at least register some social advance or establish some new principle. And, without the T.U.C., they might never have become law at all.

Members of the National Federation of Women Workers, whose amalgamation with the National Union of General and Municipal Workers was subsequently negotiated by Mary Macarthur.

# Women trade unionists on the move

Mary Macarthur, daughter of a prosperous middle-class Tory family, who became the driving force behind the Women's Trade Union League, whose work eventually became the responsibility of the T.U.C. Women's Advisory Committee. In 1919, she attended the first session of the I.L.O., in Washington, as a workers' adviser.

# The Osborne Judgement : an ominous new threat to the whole labour Movement

Lord Halsbury, a former Conservative Lord Chancellor, who was one of the Law Lords responsible for upholding the Court of Appeal's Osborne Judgement. The effect of this judgement was to make it illegal for trade unions to apply any part of their funds to the support of one of their own Parliamentary candidates, or to his maintenance if he were returned as a Member of Parliament.

Sir Charles Dilke, independent-minded Liberal politician who, with his wife, became one of the most ardent advocates of the women trade unionists' cause. From the early days when the T.U.C. had consulted him about the legal aspects of the Taff Vale Judgement he maintained a long and friendly association with the Parliamentary Committee.

THE OSBORNE Judgement arose out of a case brought, in 1908, by Mr. W.V. Osborne, secretary of the Walthamstow Branch of the Amalgamated Society of Railway Servants, who claimed that it was illegal for the A.S.R.S. to impose a "political" levy on its members for the support of its sponsored candidates who were elected to Parliament. Osborne initially lost his action; but Mr. Justice Neville's decision was later reversed by the Court of Appeal, and the House of Lords in due course confirmed that reversal, on the grounds that no provision for political activities or the political use of trade unions fund had been made in the Trade Union Act of 1876. Therefore, declared Lord Halsbury, "what is not within the ambit of that Statute is, I think, prohibited both to a corporation and a combination."

At this, a huge majority of delegates to the 1910 Trades Union Congress were up in arms, demanding that legislation to reverse the situation created by the Osborne Judgement should be introduced immediately, so that trade unions should be legally entitled to spend their own funds in whatever way they wished.

But the reversal process took some time. The situation was not, in fact, put right until 1913—and then only partially; because the Trade Union Act of that year placed a number of restrictions on a trade union's right to contribute the proceeds of its political levy to the party, or candidate, or M.P. of its choice. Meanwhile Labour M.P.s who, unlike Conservative and Liberal Members, had no private means, were enabled just to subsist by virtue of the new State payments to Members of the House of Commons, which had been introduced by Lloyd George.

John Ruskin (above) and William Morris, two of the progenitors of the idea of "Guild Socialism" and of "National Guilds", in which craftsmen would come into their own again. The objective of Guild Socialism was also workers' control of industry—but attained by evolutionary, not revolutionary, means.

"THE WORKING CLASS and the employing class have nothing in common. There can be no peace so long as hunger and want are found among millions of working people and the few, who make up the employing class, have all the good things of life. . . . These conditions can be changed and the interest of the working class upheld only by an organisation formed in such a way that all its members in any one industry, or in all industries if necessary, cease work whenever a strike or lockout is on in any department, thus making an injury to one an injury to all . . . .

"By organising industrially we are forming the structure of a new society within the shell of the old."

—from a statement by the Industrial Workers of the World or "The Wobblies" as they were commonly known.

Daniel de Leon, American Marxist, major prophet of the Industrial Workers of the World—and founder, in Britain, of the Socialist Labour Party, a fanatical body of elite Marxists, whose aims and methods were akin to those of the I.W.W.

*A mass meeting held in New York in the early 1900s by the Industrial Workers of the World: militant exponents of the creed of industrial unionism, and fervent practitioners of industrial class warfare, with no holds barred. Parallel with I.W.W. activities in the United States, Georges Sorel, the French syndicalist, had been working out the potentialities of the general strike as a political (as well as an industrial) weapon. The objectives of both syndicalism and industrial unionism were similar: workers' control of industry, leading to ultimate workers' control of the State.*

*Tom Mann, the most eloquent and militant of the British syndicalists. In 1910 he founded the Industrial Syndicalist Education League, and started publishing a monthly periodical the "Industrial Syndicalist."*

FOR MANY restless spirits who, by 1909, were becoming sceptical about the effectiveness both of parliamentary action and of the activities of the trade union movement as then constituted, the syndicalist and industrial union message had had powerful attractions. If parliamentary action had failed to get things done, how about letting un-parliamentary action have a run? If more than a thousand separate co-existent trade unions had failed to co-operate with each other inside any one industry, how about giving the syndicalist idea of "one industry one union" a try-out?

The first trade unionists to give it a partial try-out were the dockers, led by Ben Tillett, and the seamen who combined, late in 1910, to form the Transport Workers Federation (of which more on the following pages).

The next trade unionists to consider the syndicalist strategy in detail as a basis for practical action, were a group of miners' leaders, who included A. J. Cook, himself a syndicalist, and Noah Ablett. These men—in the year following the national coal strike of 1911, which led to the establishment of district minimum wages—issued a pamphlet called "The Miners' Next Step".

This pamphlet, in B. C. Roberts' words, "proposed that the miners' unions should reorganise themselves on industrial lines with a strong central direction of policy, the object of which would be to bring the industry to a standstill, with strike after strike, until the system of private ownership collapsed. Then the miners would take over the paralysed industry and re-organise it on the basis of workers' control. The ultimate aim of the authors was to see their lead followed by the trade unions in other industries".

The revolutionary implications of this syndicalist policy were in due course overwhelmingly rejected by the Trades Union Congress of 1912.

# TRIUMPH : The great dock strike of 1911

Ben Tillett, dockers' leader and one of the chief architects of the Transport Workers Federation, addressing the strikers. The successful outcome of the London dock strike, and of similar strikes in Liverpool and Manchester, seemed at first to prove the syndicalists' point.

One year after the dockers' victory, the Transport Workers' Federation are again in conflict with Lord Devenport, Chairman of the Port of London Authority, over recognition for the Federation. "O God strike Lord Devenport dead" prayed Ben Tillett on Tower Hill. But the Federation, "forgetting" as Cole and Postage wrote, "it was a Federation and not a Union overreached itself by calling a national transport strike". This was not supported. And the day—and the cause of syndicalism as such, was lost.

The tensions of the 1912 Transport Strike.

"THE effect of the transport workers' strike of this year has been disastrous, and has shown more than anything else could have done the futility of trying to fight the capitalists by what are known as Syndicalist methods."

Thus wrote Keir Hardie in 1912.

Nevertheless if syndicalism, as such, was now mouldering in the grave, industrial unionism went marching on. For, in this same year, the Amalgamated Society of Railway Servants, the General Railway Workers' Union and the United Signalmen and Pointsmen combined to form the National Union of Railwaymen. And, within two years, the combined membership of the new union had doubled itself.

Moreover, in 1913, the N.U.R. entered into a formal alliance—known as "The Triple Alliance"—with the Miners' Federation and the Transport Workers Federation, with a view to joint action for mutual assistance.

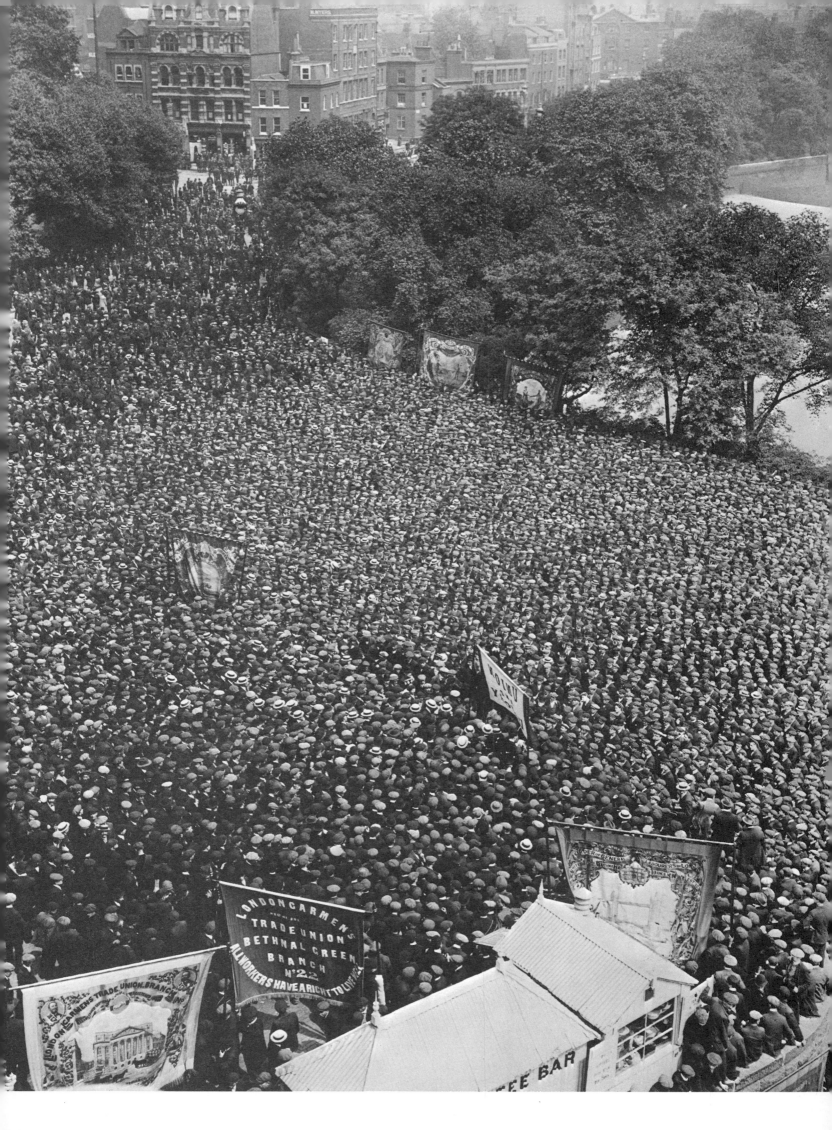

DISASTER : The great transport strike of 1912

# The Movement's two voices

George Lansbury, who took over the editorship of the " Daily Herald" in 1913, two years after its foundation. And Ramsay MacDonald, one of the newspaper's favourite targets, as seen by the Herald's cartoonist Will Dyson.

Some of the early " Daily Herald's" most brilliant and independent contributors. From left, G. K. Chesterton, Hilaire Belloc—both of them "distributists"; and G. D. H. Cole.

The " Daily Herald" (started by the London Society of Compositors as a strike sheet) was launched as a newspaper with the goodwill of the Parliamentary Committee of the T.U.C. and with the active encouragement of the Secretary of the Trades Union Congress, C. W. Bowerman, who, with W. Matkin, Secretary of the General Union of Carpenters and Joiners, at first represented the Parliamentary Committee on the Herald's board of directors. But the new paper's militant policies angered Ramsay MacDonald and his closer associates in the Labour Party. Another newspaper, the " Daily Citizen," was launched as their official organ. And in 1913, the Parliamentary Committee's support of the Herald lapsed.

Front page of the first i. of the " Daily Hera

# The Daily Herald.

No. 1.     LONDON, WEDNESDAY, JANUARY 25, 1911.     PRICE ONE HALFPENNY.

## To "ONE AND ALL."

What is this—the sound and rumour ?
What is this that all men hear,
Like the wind in hollow valleys
When the storm is drawing near ;
Like the rolling on of ocean
In the eventide of fear ?—
'Tis the People marching on.

\*   \*   \*   \*

**Men of the L.S.C.**

What nobler inspirer for the hour and the object — your modest, legitimate demand for a shorter working day—than the author of the above, that noble Old English Master Printer, William Morris, who treated his men as men, "fellow craftsmen," in that famous Kelmscott Press, down Hammersmith way ?

Yes, after many years of that tranquility which leads to sleep but not to death, "the sound and rumour " is of war !—war not of the workers' seeking, unless the worker is *ever* to receive no improvement in his everlasting drudgery.

If it is to be war, well—

We don't want to fight
But, by jingo, if we do,
We've got the men, we've got the spunk,
And we'll get the money, too !

And Englishmen who have bred sons to die for an Empire's battles abroad will not surrender their right like a horde of starveling Asiatics at the behest of those who on the hustings prate of being the "workers' friend " !

Men, every Trade Union of England is saying, "Though betrayed, they will not betray "; and every Trade Union in Europe, America and the Colonies is watching you. "Quit ye like men ! "

Capital may be strong, but manhood is stronger. And the Old Guard never dies, and never surrenders.

The Press may ignore your claims, the Pulpit ignore your struggle. What of it ? Every refusal of such palpable right as yours—ours —sets men thinking ; and when men are set thinking by injustice, other things, hitherto undreamt of, follow.

"Ask and ye shall receive." Ye have asked —to be rejected. Very well, then, in the name of Christ, "KNOCK and it *shall* be opened unto you." Be determined. Money will follow, if needed. The L.S.C. has a world-wide, honoured name.

One thing—this (something the " Liberal " newspapers will not publish from me ) : Those big firms who oppose us should remember that their splendid fortunes for years past have been made from Government printing. The Government gives the 48 hours to the direct employees everywhere. Why, then, are the Printers who do the work of the State refused *their* 48-hour week ? Let the Employers remember that they have a privilege—London has no Government Printing House. In other lands the Government does its own work. Two can play at war. If the Masters are provocatively wicked, others can be. There is a Labour Party in the House, and it holds supreme power.

On we march, then—we, the workers,
And the rumour that ye hear
Is the blended soul of battle
And deliverance drawing near,
For the hope of every creature
Is the banner that we bear :

**50—48.**

Yours, fellow workers, in the hope that conquers.     W. F. REAN.

## STRIKING PARAGRAPHS.

WE have arrived. At last we have a daily paper of our own. If we differ at all from the orthodox daily press, it will be in the fact that we shall give the *correct* position of affairs day by day.

—: o : —

We ask our readers to be kind, and excuse our imperfections. We have met the usual difficulties that always attend the production of a first number. Still, we have arrived.

—: o : —

The necessity for our existence was brought very close to our mind yesterday when we took up our daily paper and found there the report of a case in which a member of the L.S.C. was the plaintiff. That case went against the trade union. Because it went against us a long report was given of the case, with headings and sub-headings to match. This is pretty Fanny's way. Some time since we contested a similar case, which we won. On that occasion the daily press contented themselves with a short notice of the hearing or omitted it entirely. But this is pretty Fanny's way.

—: o : —

In another column we print the first instalment of a series of letters written by Mr. Joseph Causton to the members of the London Master Printers' Association. They form interesting reading. As the letters proceed our readers will see how the tone has to be changed according to the developments of the dispute.

—: o : —

We offer no comment upon the taste displayed in the writing thereof, but the letters furnish evidence of the strenuous efforts made by the Chairman of the Association to make his members " hang together." The present position indicates, however, that they are hanging separately.

—: o : —

We are going strong. The returns which have come in have been highly satisfactory. It is not our intention to suppress facts. As soon as we have tabulated the results, we shall issue a list of the houses which have conceded the terms, and others which have not. Mr. Causton has anticipated us in publishing a list of houses which have not yet conceded the terms, and knowing that moderation is not his chief characteristic, we are delighted to find that he can only account for fourteen.

—: o : —

We reprint his letter in another part of this issue. Needless to add, many of these firms will be captured before the next fortnight. Meanwhile we can afford to be satisfied with the houses already won.

We are surprised to see, in one of the letters issued by the Master Printers' Association, that employers who concede the men's terms may be made to suffer for their temerity. Is this a threat ?

—: o : —

One of the most conspicuous features of the dispute has been the loyalty of the L.S.C. members. The notices have been tendered almost without exception. In only one instance has it come to our knowledge that certain members of the chapel failed to respond to the call. The proprietors of that establishment have decided that they will convert the establishment into an " open house." Here let it be known, once and for all, that the question of the " open house " will be fought as strenuously as the hours question itself. Members who have tendered notices will not withdraw them if any non-union man is retained in the department. Chapel Officers should make a note of this and act accordingly.

—: o : —

Our members must be prepared for certain methods of deception that are being practised. To one office, at least, a bogus telegram was sent to the Father of the Chapel ordering him to cancel notices—a trick of a most discreditable character. Forewarned is forearmed. Members receiving letters or telegrams subject to suspicion should take steps to verify them at headquarters.

—: o : —

A rumour has also got abroad, circulated no doubt with an object, to the effect that small offices are exempt from the instructions. Another canard.

## REPORT OF CONFERENCE

HELD ON TUESDAY, JANUARY 10, 1911.
Representatives of the National Printing and Kindred Trades Federation :—Messrs. C. W. Bowerman, M.P. (President), H. Skinner (Treasurer), J. Templeton (Vice-President), J. Kelly, R. Barnes, H. W. Hewes, A. Evans and Geo. D. Kelley (Secretary).
Representatives of the Master Printers :— Federation of Master Printers : Messrs. R. H. H. Baird, W. Wright Bemrose, Harry Cooke, E. G. Arnold, W. N. Turner, C. Bewick Ward, J. E. T Allen and J. Sever   Linotype Users' Association : Messrs. Meredith T. Whittaker, G. E Stembridge, W. K. Mackay and E. Taylor Thomlinson (Secretary and Joint Secretary of Federation of Master Printers). London Master Printers' Association : Messrs. Joseph Causton, Alfred F. Blades, J. J. Keliher, C. R. Harrison, and A. Causby Smith (Acting Secretary). Federation Northern Newspaper Owners : Messrs A. R Byles and Frank Bird (Secretary). Federation Southern Newspaper Owners : Mr. D. Duncan   Irish Newspaper Society : Mr. C W Henderson.   Lancashire Newspaper Society : Mr W. Roger.   Scotland Mr. J. Thomlinson (Glasgow).

On the motion of Mr. C. W. Bowerman, the chair was occupied by Mr. M. T. Whittaker, and Mr. C W. Bowerman was immediately afterwards voted to the vice-chair.

### CHAIRMAN'S OPENING SPEECH.

The Chairman : Gentlemen, this is the first opportunity some of us on this side of the table have had of seeing some of you gentlemen on the other side ; and I trust that, before we disperse, you will entertain a favourable opinion of those of us who may differ from

# Nothing sacred: Will Dyson's blistering pen

*"**Trades Union officials** (to the Boy-Who-Would-Grow-Up): 'Here, I say, think of us. This Growth has got to stop'. (Dedicated to the Officials at Unity House and their pathetic efforts to check this modern tendency on the part of the Rank and File to outgrow Institutions.)"*

*"**An impression of Bill Haywood**, of the Industrial Workers of the World, of America, who returned yesterday to the States. He took with him the good wishes of all devoted to the cause of the Greater Unionism, but we understand that the capitalists of Great Britain are bearing up very well against the loss of his society."*

*"**The heavy parent**: 'My dear, if the violence of those Militants succeeds in establishing the excellent principle of the deportation of the politically undesirable, well, I for one will feel that they have not lived in vain.'"*

*"**The spirit of armaments** (to the peaceful peasants of Tweedledom and Tweedledeedom): 'What, you go short of food that I may wax fat? What would safeguard for you even that meagre food supply were I not here to prevent you tearing it wolf-like from the other's jaws?'"*

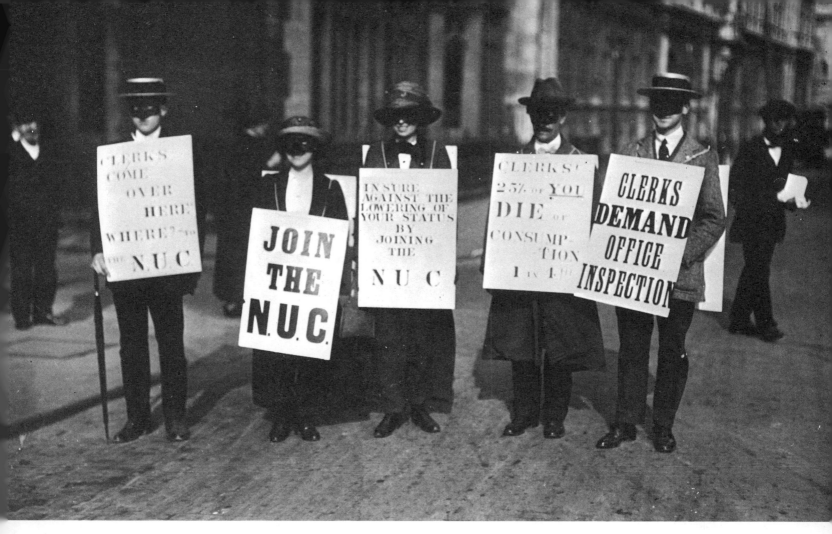

*Autumn, 1913. Men and women of the National Union of Clerks, on the march from Temple Steps to a meeting in Hyde Park wearing masks to prevent victimisation.*

# on the eve of the first world war

*May 1914. The Suffragettes' assault on Buckingham Palace. In three months' time, both the suffragette problem and the Irish Home Rule problem, which had been pre-occupying government and people alike, were to be pushed to the back of everyone's mind by the outbreak of a war which the large and apparently powerful trade unions of Britain, Germany and France were powerless to prevent; and which, in the event, they felt impelled to support.*

*"There's a long, long trail a-winding, unto the land of our dreams, where the nightingales are singing,. And the white moon beams . . ."*

THE ACTUAL OUTBREAK of war caught the labour and trade union Movements of Europe off balance. As late as August 2nd a mass meeting addressed by British labour leaders in Trafalgar Square had passed a resolution proclaiming that " The Government of Britain should rigidly decline to engage in war, but should confine itself to efforts to bring about peace as speedily as possible."

Two days later, the Kaiser's armies invaded Belgium, and almost everyone in Britain felt a shock of indignation and repugnance. The conference that had been called for August 5th at the House of Commons by Arthur Henderson and C. W. Bowerman, at which representatives of the Parliamentary Committee were present, when faced now with the actuality of war, proposed the setting-up of a War Emergency Workers' National Committee to protect

# The first "Great war for civilisation": workers of all lands, united in a mutual massacre

*A cartoon drawn by Ed. Battle, and published by the "Daily Herald" in February, 1914. The caption reads "**Peace on earth** Being offered as a supplement to the designs, pointing out the advantages of Life in the Army, which our War Office is now circulating." When war broke out six months later, the Herald mourned the happening; but the newspaper did not start to oppose it until December, 1914.*

workers as far as possible from war's economic effects.

Ramsay MacDonald, who had always insisted that if war broke out both sides would be to blame, then felt impelled to resign as leader of the Labour Party. He was succeeded by Arthur Henderson, who believed that—now that the war was on—the labour Movement must play its full part in helping to win it.

The Parliamentary Committee of the T.U.C. held the same views; and, on August 24th, the Committee declared itself in favour of urging all unions to observe an industrial truce for the duration.

Everything possible, it affirmed, should be done to bring existing disputes to an end, and to forestall or settle any future disputes which might lead to stoppages.

# The wartime revolution in trade union conditions

"THE GOVERNMENT found itself, within a year, under the necessity of asking the trade unions for the unprecedented sacrifice of the relinquishment, for the duration of the war, of the entire network of 'Trade Union Conditions' which had been slowly built up by generations of effort for the protection of the workman's standard of life", wrote the Webbs.

"This enormous draft on the patriotism of the rank and file could only be secured by enlisting the support of the official representatives of the Trade Union world, by according to them a unique and unprecedented place as the diplomatic representatives of the wage-earning class.

"In the famous Treasury Conference of February, 1915, the capitalist employers were ignored, and the principal Ministers of the Crown negotiated directly with the authorised representatives of the whole Trade Union World . . . ."

The Treasury Agreement—which provided for an undertaking by the unions not to strike while the war was still on, and which laid it down that unsettled disputes must be sent to arbitration—was indeed a landmark. But the "authorised representatives" (which included a representative of the T.U.C. Parliamentary Committee) were not empowered to commit "the whole Trade Union World". In fact, the miners withdrew their representatives on the first day of that three day Treasury meeting with Lloyd George, the Chancellor of the Exchequer, and Walter Runciman, the President of the Board of Trade. And the Amalgamated Society of Engineers signed the agreement only after seeking, and receiving, separate reassurances that trade practices would be suspended only in firms concerned with war production, and that in those same firms excess profits would be limited.

*John Hodge, of the steel smelters, whom Lloyd George on becoming Prime Minister in 1916 appointed to be Britain's first Minister of Labour.*

*A woman munition worker gauging shell cases. By the "Shells and Fuses Agreement" of 1915, engineering unions and employers had agreed to the recommendations of Sir George Askwith's Treasury Committee on Production, whereby dilution of labour was to be accepted until the end of the war.*

*Robert Smillie, a Scottish miners' leader who, as President of the Miners Federation in 1914, had promoted the Triple Alliance of Miners, Railwaymen and Transport Workers, leads a wartime protest meeting against the war-profiteers. In contrast to profits, real wages actually fell in the course of the first world war. For, though money wages were roughly doubled between 1914 and 1918, the cost of living rose, during the same period, by 120 per cent.*

# The TUC's contribution to the war effort

DURING the first World War, the T.U.C. participated in the administration of government at a number of different levels. The Cabinet Minister who, from the earliest days, saw most clearly the desirability of such participation was Lloyd George. In 1915, as Minister of Munitions, he accepted an invitation to address the Trades Union Congress in person, about the working of the Munitions Act. When, in December 1916, he succeeded Asquith as Prime Minister, he immediately gave Arthur Henderson a seat in the War Cabinet; created a Ministry of Labour, and made John Hodge, Secretary of the Steel Smelters, the Minister; and gave G. N. Barnes, of the Amalgamated Society of Engineers, the post of Minister of Pensions. He also quickly acceded to the T.U.C.'s long-standing demands for public control of mines, shipping and food distribution. In fact, Lloyd George had always been convinced of the importance of T.U.C. support of the Government's war effort and not least because of the man-power problem.

At other levels of wartime administration, trade union participation came to be extraordinarily wide-spread. Members of the Parliamentary Committee and other trade union representatives served on many of the 2,000 or so advisory committees that were set up by Government departments to assist in the prosecution of the war effort.

This involvement of the Movement in the administration of government did not survive the end of the war. And it was to take another war to bring it fully back to life.

# Rise of the shop stewards

"THE FIRST world war led to a very rapid development of the shop stewards' movement," wrote G. D. H. Cole. "Under war conditions, changes in workshop practice were continually being made . . . . up-grading of less skilled workers to skilled jobs, breaking up jobs previously done by skilled workers into their skilled and less skilled components, extended employment of female labour, and so on. These changes had to be introduced by negotiation at the workshop level; for they were far too many and diverse to be handled by full-time Trade Union officials or by district negotiation. They came to be handled mainly by shop stewards and shop stewards' committees."

"The shop steward" wrote R. Page Arnot "was originally a minor official appointed from the men in a particular workshop and charged with the duty of seeing that all the Trade Union contributions were paid. He had other small duties. But gradually, as the branch got more and more out of touch with the men in the shop, these men came to look to the official who was on the spot to represent their grievances. . . . In some big industrial concerns, composed of a number of workshops, the committees of stewards from the various shops very largely took over the whole conduct of negotiations and arrangement of shop conditions."

This was especially true of the engineering and ship building industries and of the North East, Clydeside and Coventry areas, where the more militant trade unionists began to look to the shop stewards as a permanent alternative leadership.

Four phases
of "The war
to make...

...the world
safe for
democracy!"

# The impact of the Russian revolution on the British labour Movement

*Between the February and October Revolutions: the riots of July, 1917.*

*After the February, 1917, revolution in Russia, Kerensky, who eventually became head of the Provisional Government, reviews his men. The British labour Movement welcomed the new Government; and Will Thorne, a member of the Parliamentary Committee of the T.U.C. was one of the delegates appointed by the Labour Party to convey its good wishes and those of the T.U.C. to Moscow, and to invite the Russian trade unions, if any could be found, to send a fraternal delegate to Congress.*

SOON AFTER Will Thorne's return from his Moscow visit in 1917 with the news that there was no trade union centre in Russia, the Parliamentary Committee of the T.U.C. proposed sending two of its members to assist the Russians in the task of strengthening and organising its trade union Movement. But the Provisional Russian Government did not react to this proposal—though it did indicate its willingness to participate in an International Socialist Conference to be held in Stockholm, at which workers' war and peace aims could be concerted.

Lloyd George sent Arthur Henderson to Russia on a mission of enquiry to investigate the desirability of British trade union and Labour Party participation in such a conference. Henderson reported back in favour of such participation. And Lloyd George immediately vetoed the whole project.

Later, in the summer of 1920, when Lloyd George was backing the Poles in their anti-Soviet crusade, the dockers, with Ernest Bevin's encouragement, declined to load the Jolly George with arms destined for the Polish armed forces. The Trades Union Congress and the Labour Party supported the dockers' stand.

Shortly afterwards, when it looked as though Lloyd George was going to intervene actively with massive ground support for the Poles, Congress and Labour Party set up a "Council of Action" to organise a strike to stop the war. Lloyd George thereupon did another about-turn; and British support for the Poles petered out.

Meanwhile, the T.U.C. had been reviewing the role of the British trade union Movement in international affairs, and "the desirability of making the Parliamentary Committee the British centre for dealing with international Trade Union matters." In July 1918, a conference of representatives of trade unions that were affiliated to the international federations resolved that the Parliamentary Committee should be requested to set up an international trade union bureau for the collection, and dissemination to unions affiliated to the T.U.C., of statistical and other information bearing on relevant international matters. The Parliamentary Committee was also urged to foster a closer association between British and other trade union movements, not least that of the United States. For when, earlier in 1918, the Allied Labour and Socialist Conference presided over by J. W. Ogden, the then Chairman of the Parliamentary Committee, had endorsed the main points of the British Movement's declaration of war aims, which had been greatly influenced by the declarations of President Wilson, the American Federation of Labour had been conspicuous by its absence.

In the following year, the Parliamentary Committee, after being called into consultation by George Barnes (who was by then one of Britain's representatives at the Peace Conference), about a projected International Labour Organisation, contributed a number of improvements to the British draft memorandum which was destined to become, with slight modifications, the blueprint for the I.L.O.

In August 1918, the London police suddenly went on strike, in an effort to get recognition of their union, the Police and Prison Officers' Union which had been founded by Ex-Inspector Symes. One year later the union issued a national strike call; but only the London police (above) and some of the Liverpool force responded. And the union was smashed.

# The pains of peace

SOON AFTER the Armistice of 1918 the Labour Party pulled its Ministers out of the Government, and prepared to fight the imminent "khaki election" on the basis of their recent policy statement "Labour and the New Social Order", as "the party of the workers by hand and brain". But they cut little ice against Lloyd George's "homes for heroes" rhetoric, which procured the return of the Coalition Government with a colossal majority.

Nevertheless, nearly sixty Labour M.P.s, of whom some 50 were trade union nominees, did get into Parliament.

The Conservative-dominated Government, in accordance with the wartime agreement, passed a Restoration of Pre-War Practices Act, and abolished the compulsory arbitration regulations that had been introduced in the war industries. Instead, a permanent Industrial Court was set up to deal with disputes brought to it by the voluntary agreement of employers and unions.

At the same time Whitley Councils were initiated in the Civil Service, the Royal Dockyards and the Post Office. The Union of Post Office Workers was deemed to have shown symptons of syndicalist fever. One of the Union's declared objectives, in fact, was: "the organisation of Post Office Workers into a comprehensive industrial union with a view to the Service being ultimately conducted and managed by the Guild."

As long ago as the Trades Union Congress of 1916, Harry Gosling, as president of Congress, had spoken presciently of the post-war situation. "... we hope for something better than a mere avoidance of unemployment and strikes" he said. "We are tired of war in the industrial field. The British Workman cannot quietly submit to an autocratic government of the conditions of his own life. He will not take 'Prussianism' lying down, even in the dock, the factory, or the mine. Would it not be possible for the employers of this country, on the conclusion of peace, when we have rid ourselves of the restrictive legislation to which we have submitted for war purposes, to agree to put their businesses on a new footing by admitting the workmen to some participation, not in profits but in control."

*J. H. Whitley, Speaker of the House of Commons. On the implementation of the recommendations of his 1916 Committee, which had included Robert Smillie and J. R. Clynes among its members, and which was in many ways ahead of its time, reposed some of the chief hopes of industrial peace in the immediate post-war years. Among the Committee's recommendations were those for the setting up of Joint Industrial Councils and Joint Works Committees; for a permanent court of arbitration; for the statutory regulation of wages in industries where collective bargaining was non-existent; and for enlarged powers for Ministers of Labour to inquire into industrial disputes.*

# An unforgettable new face appears upon the troubled industrial scene

*Ernest Bevin in 1920. His masterly advocacy of the London dockers' case, which had been referred to arbitration with the consent of both unions and employers in accordance with the Industrial Courts Act of 1919, earned him the nickname of "the dockers' K.C." Through him the dockers won considerable wage increases and a recommendation for decasualisation which was put into full effect just short of 50 years later in 1967.*

*Members of the General Council of the Trades Union Congress, with some of the staff, in the year when the Council was brought into being in order to "co-ordinate the industrial action" of all unions.*

# 1921 : The General Council of the TUC replaces the Parliamentary Committee

*J. H. Thomas, Railwaymen's leader, who came in for much of the blame for calling off—at the last moment, on Black Friday, April 15, 1921—a sympathetic strike of railwaymen and transport workers in support of the miners, who had been locked out by the coal-owners for rejecting their proposals for substantial wage cuts. This "betrayal" of the miners finally buried the Triple Alliance.*

EVER SINCE 1916, forward-looking spirits had been casting around for some form of organisation to provide the T.U.C. with a more effective instrument than the Parliamentary Committee for the promotion of common action by the whole trade union Movement on general and national questions.

In his presidential address to the 1916 Trades Union Congress, Harry Gosling had said:—

"The Trades Union Congress is without question the largest and most influential body in reflecting the aims and aspirations of Labour, not only in Great Britain, but in the whole world. Most of us whose connection with the Congress as delegates goes back for 20 years or more know how the work has increased in volume and importance, and yet no real provision has been made to meet the increase. Whilst we have improved in our office accommodation the staff is practically the same; the

affiliation fees which were fixed fourteen years ago are still in operation, and only amount to a payment of 1d per annum for every three members affiliated. Fortunately we have one of the best men in the Movement as our Secretary, C. W. Bowerman, to whom nothing but praise is due for the devoted way in which he serves us. He, together with his clerk, compose the whole of the staff employed in this great work!

"We see on all hands that the employers are hastening to put matters right so far as their own particular interests are concerned. The employer's interests in the near future will be protected by powerfully organised and well directed associations. This Congress will have to undertake still greater responsibilities. Its work will be even more important and far reaching in character than anything it has yet attempted. The work of the Parliamentary Committee will be greater than ever. Its offices and its staff

## The mines for the nation

A BRIEF but spectacular boom followed the Armistice, generating gigantic profits for the manufacturers concerned—a fact which did not escape the notice of the trade unions, whose own strength had increased during the war years from 4,145,000 members in 1914, to 6,533,000 members in 1918. The Wages Temporary Regulation Act for which the unions had lobbied during the last months of the war, provided a temporary shield against wage cuts; but many shop stewards and militant

unionists felt that, with large profits and little unemployment, they could do better than simply hold what they had.

Unofficial strikes erupted in Yorkshire, on the North-East Coast on the Clyde and in Belfast. In Glasgow, police were brought in to control the strikers; but in London and Liverpool the police themselves went on strike. As did many of the troops, returning home to Folkestone and Dover from the slaughterfields of Flanders, on failing to recognise the officially promised "land fit for heroes to live in".

More serious, perhaps, for the Government, was the probability of an official national coal strike, arising out of the unsatisfied demands of the Miners' Federation for higher wages, a six-hour day, and the nationalisation of coal-mining—with a degree of workers' control of the industry exercised through Miners' Federation representatives. The question of whether or not the mines

should be handed back to private ownership now became a major issue.

The Government in alarm reached for a Commission: half of whose members—it was conceded, in order to avert a strike,—should be nominated by the Miners' Federation. The president was to be Mr. Justice Sankey.

The Sankey Commission, which included Sidney Webb, R. H. Tawney, and the miners' leader Robert Smillie among its members, though divided on various matters, came down as a majority on the side of the principle that "the State ownership of coal mines be accepted." A principle which, predictably, proved repugnant and unacceptable to Lloyd George's Coalition Government, which duly passed the mines back into private control in 1921. Meanwhile the T.U.C. and the Labour Party had started a crusade for the nationalisation of coal, under the banner slogan "The Mines for the Nation."

must be added to, and the affiliation fees—if they are not sufficient—must be increased. We must not be satisfied until organised Labour is as important in its greater and more national aspects as any Department of State, with its own block of offices and Civil Servants, commodious and well appointed."

Harry Gosling then mooted the appointment of a sub-committee of the Parliamentary Committee to examine the alternative possibilities.

The next big stride forward was taken in the autumn of 1919, after a strike by the N.U.R. which was settled on satisfactory terms as a result of the efforts of a Mediation Committee representing other unions affected by the strike. The success of this operation pointed the need for what B. C. Roberts called a "permanent General Staff" for the trade union Movement. And the Parliamentary Committee set up a Co-ordination Committee to consider how this could best be achieved.

In due course, the Co-ordination Committee produced its report and recommendations for the creation of a General Council of the T.U.C., with responsibilities far wider than those with which the Parliamentary Committee had been endowed. Apart from keeping watch on all industrial movements and co-ordinating industrial action, the General Council would be expected to use their influence to settle actual or potential inter-union disputes ; they would also help trade unions to organise and would enter into relations with the trade union Movements of other countries.

These recommendations aroused in various unions some anxieties about their future freedom of action. To assuage these anxieties the Parliamentary Committee consented to a preamble paragraph which read: " Subject to the necessary safeguards to secure the complete autonomy of the unions and federations affiliated to Congress." This meant, in effect, that the General Council were to be given larger responsibilities than the Parliamentary Committee, without the increased co-ordinating powers which would be necessary to enable them wholly to meet these responsibilities. The point was immediately grasped by Ernest Bevin who, while diplomatically commenting that "there is no finality in our conception of organisation" declared forthrightly: "What I want to do is to create a greatly improved equipment and efficiency."

The General Council eventually came into being along the pragmatic lines already adumbrated, in 1921. In addition to all its other functions, the General Council were now to set up, in conjunction with the Labour Party Executive, joint departments for research and information, press and publicity, and international matters,

*Harry Gosling, secretary of the Amalgamated Society of Watermen, Lightermen and Bargemen (and later to become President of the Transport and General Workers' Union) who in his Presidential address to the 1916 T.U.C. Congress set out the case for a strengthening of the Movement to meet the challenges of the post-war world.*

*Walter Citrine, one of the most eminent, authoritative and influential leaders in the history of the T.U.C. He first attracted attention when in 1919, as a youngish and then relatively militant trade unionist, he attacked the Parliamentary Committee of the T.U.C. for giving only half-hearted backing to the demands of the Police Officers' Union. In 1925 he became assistant general secretary, and in 1926, general secretary of the T.U.C.*

which were to be run by paid and full-time officials.

Such vastly increased responsibilities and activities called, in the view of Gosling and others, for the institution of a full-time chairman of the General Council, to be elected by Congress. Some unions felt that this would be putting too much power into the hands of the T.U.C. at the possible expense of individual unions. For the same sort of reasons, the same group of union leaders secured the rejection of a resolution which would have given the T.U.C. authority to try and achieve a just settlement of a major dispute before there was an actual stoppage of work.

Nevertheless, the General Council played an influential part, both by convening conferences of unions and by giving moral support, in the forthcoming renewed movement towards amalgamation and the formation of general unions. (It was perhaps significant that the foundation of the Amalgamated Engineering Union in 1920, and its subsequent refusal of the employers' proposed wage reductions in the following year, led to the national engineering lock-out of 1922.) The trend towards the amalgamation of existing unions, which had reappeared with the foundation of the British Iron, Steel and Kindred Trades Association in 1917 was strengthened in 1922 with the momentous Bevin-inspired merger of fourteen separate unions into the Transport and General Workers Union. Amalgamations were also taking place in the Civil Service: the Union of Post Office Workers was formed in 1920 and by 1926, unions in the Post Office had recruited 100,000 out of 190,000 postal workers; whilst on the clerical side a number of union amalgamations led in 1922 to the setting up of the Civil

Service Clerical Association. In 1918, the National Amalgamated Union of Life Assurance Workers developed out of the National Union of Insurance Workers which, like the Association of Engineering and Shipbuilding Draughtsmen, had come into being around 1913. Even more significant was the creation, in 1920, of the National Federation of Professional Workers, whose representatives in 1923 joined with the T.U.C. in forming a Consultative Committee—known to-day as the T.U.C. Non-manual Workers' Advisory Committee. Another amalgamation brought into being the National Union of General and Municipal Workers.

This was at a time when the trade union Movement as a whole was losing members at a frightening rate. Total membership figures, which in 1918 stood at 6,533,000, had moved up to 8,348,000 by 1920. But by 1922 they were down to 5,625,000. This situation seemed to call for at least some measures of consolidation.

Meanwhile, between 1918 and 1921, the T.U.C.'s income had jumped from £9,000 to £37,000. This enabled the general secretary to begin to appoint specialist staff of the kind so long advocated by the Webbs.

In 1925, the General Council proposed to the Congress that the current arrangements with the Labour Party, under which Joint Press and Publicity, Research and Information and International Departments were maintained, should now be terminated. The Council considered that the now rapidly expanding work of the T.U.C. could only be carried on effectively if the General Council had entire control of their own Publicity, Research and International Departments. By the following year, this had been accomplished.

# 1924: Labour in office . .

*January, 1924. With Liberal Parliamentary support, Labour comes to office, though not to power. And Ramsay MacDonald dedicates himself to looking, and acting, like a truly traditional Prime Minister.*

THE TWENTY-STRONG Cabinet of Ramsay MacDonald's Government, which had been installed largely by the votes of trade unionists, included only seven trade union men. As a minority Government, there were severe restrictions on what it could have hoped to achieve during its short term of office; but its apparent acceptance of "orthodox economics" disappointed many of its supporters, and particularly the miners.

As G. D. H. Cole wrote: "The struggles of 1921 and 1926, with the Mineworkers on both occasions in the centre of the battle, were in effect a challenge to the view that Trade Unions must bow to 'economic laws', as believed in and acted upon by their betters. On both occasions the miners went on strike, not so much against the mine-owners as against deflation, or rather its consequences. They were staking out a claim that it was someone's duty—in effect, the Government's—to see to it that living wages should be paid and employment maintained at a satisfactory level; and J. M. Keynes, challenging the prevalent economic orthodoxy, reinforced their claim with arguments which set a whole generation of economists, and even bankers, by the ears."

# rade unionists left out in the cold

A miner's wife on a routine visit to the pawnshop in the early 1920's: one of the millions of "workers by hand and brain" on whom the advent of the first Labour Government had no effect at all—except to disillusion them. All MacDonald's governments were destined to behave as though unemployment was an Act of God arising out of that other unfortunate and immutable Act of God—the trade cycle, and its periodic tidal waves of deflation.

J. M. Keynes. One man who knew better than most that the trade cycle was not an Act of God, and that unemployment could be cured by man. By 1930 Keynes had the ear of the General Council and had increasing influence upon the policies of the trade union Movement.

*An armoured car escorts a food convoy through the streets of strike-bound London —despite the fact that, from the beginning of the strike, the T.U.C. had made it clear that foodstuffs would be allowed free passage.*

# The gold standard road to the general strike

THE SHORT-LIVED Labour Government had more or less consistently cold-shouldered the T.U.C. and its leaders. And the Conservative Government, which took office in November 1924, saw no reason not to continue this conveniently cool policy, and preferably improve on it. So when, in 1925, the dictates of "orthodox economics" impelled Winston Churchill, as Chancellor of the Exchequer, to land Britain back on the gold standard at the old pre-war parity—a move which inevitably played havoc with British exports, Stanley Baldwin, as Prime Minister, was quick to spell out the logical consequences:— "All workers in this country have got to take reductions in wages". The coal-owners demanded that the miners should do just that, and that they should accept, also, a return to the eight-hour day.

The Miners' Federation leaders sought the assistance of the General Council of the T.U.C., who successfully urged the railwaymen and the transport workers —the miners' old partners in the Triple Alliance—to agree in principle that, if it came to a crunch, they would refuse to move any coal, stocks of which were now superabundant.

At this, Baldwin recoiled, and introduced a stalling subsidy to sustain miners' wages until the Royal Commission which he now set up, devoid of miners' representation, under Sir Herbert Samuel's chairmanship, should have time to report. The eventual report recommended substantial wage cuts, such as the miners' leaders, notably the veteran syndicalist, A. J. Cook, were in no mood to accept. The General Council of the T.U.C. then took a hand at attempting to negotiate a fair settlement of the miners' claims with the exceedingly self-confident Government.

But the Government, which for many months had been making precautionary strike-breaking preparations, saw no reason to consider any concessions. Nevertheless the General Council had almost managed to negotiate a satisfactory settlement when an incident at the "Daily Mail", where the machine men refused to print the leading article attacking the strike, gave the Government a pretext for breaking off discussions, on May 3rd. On May 1st, the miners lock-out had started. And on May 4th there began the general strike —as it was commonly called—for which the General Council had indeed been making precautionary preparations, but only during the previous few days.

In fact, the "general strike" was not, in any real sense, general. (The trade unions themselves preferred the name "national strike".) The only principal unions initially called out in support of the miners were those of the railwaymen, the transport workers, the builders, the iron and steel workers—and the printers, engineers and shipyard workers were called out after the first week, when it was almost all over bar the recriminations.

The Government, with the help of some people at the "Morning Post," contrived to print and publish an official news-sheet called the "British Gazette". The General Council, none of whose mem-

## Memo to all despatch riders

DESPATCH riders provided practically the only means of intercommunication between the T.U.C. headquarters at 32 Eccleston Square, London, and the local strike committees and "councils of action" throughout the rest of Britain. But, in the first few days, it became clear that the despatch riders' telegrams were being intercepted and their telephone messages tapped. So, on May 11, H. H. Elvin, Chairman of the General Purposes Committee of the T.U.C. General Council, issued a code to be used by despatch riders when telephoning-in their reports. The following are some samples of the code:—

### Police

| | |
|---|---|
| Police .. .. .. .. | beauty |
| Police baton charges .. .. | beautify |
| Troops in control of .. .. | beautiful |
| Troops fired on crowds .. .. | beautifully |
| Persons injured by police or troops (give number) .. .. great |
| Persons killed by police or troops (give number) .. .. greater |

### Railwaymen

| | |
|---|---|
| Railwaymen .. .. .. .. .. .. rain |
| Railwaymen serious increase of blacklegging against .. .. rainless |
| Railwaymen wavering .. .. .. .. .. raining |
| Railwaymen returning to work .. .. .. .. .. rained |

"Have come out".............name the union or unions and add the suffix................more (e.g. cartermore, electricmore)

### Pickets

| | |
|---|---|
| Pickets .. .. .. .. | play |
| Pickets arrested .. .. .. | played |
| Pickets injured (give number) .. | great play |
| Pickets killed (give number) .. | greater play |

### Strike committee

| | |
|---|---|
| Strike committee .. .. .. .. .. .. | sweat |
| Strike committee raided .. .. .. .. .. | sweating |
| Strike committee arrested .. .. .. .. .. | sweated |
| Strike committee short of funds .. .. .. .. | unsweat |
| Strike committee police in charge of premises .. .. | sweat beauty |

bers were allowed to broadcast on the B.B.C., retaliated with their own newspaper "The British Worker." And it soon became clear that the sympathetic strikes were close on 100 per cent solid.

What was much less clear to the strikers and their leaders was the question of who among them was entitled to arrive at a settlement of the dispute. Should the Miners Federation have the final word, or the T.U.C. General Council.

"The only question at stake—except those connected with the legal and political aspects of the conflict—was that of the terms under which the miners were to work, "wrote G. D. H. Cole. However, "the General Council insisted on its right to act on behalf of the entire movement: the Miners' leaders insisted that they were solely responsible to their own Delegate Conference and could not go against its wishes. Neither side would budge, and in the end this was the ground on which the General Council called off the strike, leaving the miners to fight on alone."

*A blackleg bus, adorned with a policeman on its bonnet. A number of undergraduates and others had a go at driving the occasional bus; but they had much less success with locomotives.*

*The Chiswick bus depot invites all its employees to register again for work on the Monday following the end of the general strike.*

# The strikers go back to work
# and the Tories reach for the law

IN THE YEARS following the General Strike, the Tory Trade Disputes and Trade Unions Act dealt both wings of the labour Movement a stinging left and right. Apart from making general strikes illegal, this law required the Civil Service unions to dissociate themselves completely from both the T.U.C. and the Labour Party. And it enforced a contracting-in system (instead of the contracting-out system) for contributing to political funds.

For good measure, the Conservative Government also took a swipe at the unemployed, who were henceforth to be deprived of benefit if they were deemed not to be "genuinely seeking work." A neatly-timed Tory move; because the deflation ordained by orthodox economics and similar Acts of God had ensured that now there was practically no work to seek.

*The men—and women— who ran the general strike assembled in the library at the Countess of Warwick's home which was then being considered as a trade union educational centre.*

*In the wilderness of the workless years between the two world wars trade unionists in general and the T.U.C. in particular were continuously fighting to hang on to the gains made in the earlier part of the century. In the main, however, it was a losing battle. The T.U.C. was more often than not ignored by successive Governments as trade unionists were by employers. Yet confronted with this depressing and seemingly irrevocable weakening of trade union influence, the T.U.C. was doing much of the groundwork for the policies on economic and social change which were to mark the post-war period.*

# The TUC's formative years and the figh

DURING most of this third phase of its development, the T.U.C.'s contacts with governments were more intermittent and its official relations with governments more distant than they had been during most of the previous period, when both Lloyd George and Winston Churchill had been quick to grasp the importance of bringing the representatives of organised labour into regular consultation and even—during the first world war—into active participation in the administration of government.

Now, when the second Labour Government of 1929-31 began to find itself in a tight corner, Ramsay MacDonald and Philip Snowden showed themselves to be much less receptive to the T.U.C.'s views. They did eventually listen to the T.U.C.'s constructive proposals for combating the 1931 economic crisis; but they did not allow those proposals to deflect them at all from going ahead with the wholesale "economy" cuts that had been proposed to them by the apostles of orthodox finance.

The National Government which followed did break new ground by inviting two representatives of the T.U.C. to attend the Imperial Economic Conference at Ottawa in 1932, as advisers. And, throughout the next seven years, there were a number of contacts between individual Cabinet Ministers and representatives of the T.U.C. on specific measures of legislation affecting working people.

But on the major issues of trade and industry, poverty and unemployment, collective security and rearmament, peace and war, the T.U.C. during the 1930's found it almost impossible to get a serious hearing from the National Government, the Baldwin Government or the Chamberlain Government.

Ever since the General Strike, Conservative Governments had instinctively treated the representatives of organised labour as men on the outside looking in. Even when the second world war broke out, the Chamberlain Government's attitude inhibited the initial work of the Ministry of Labour's newly-formed National Joint Advisory Committee, which was supposed to assist the Minister, Ernest Brown, in formulating policy about such things as wage-control, compulsory arbitration, and direction of labour. When the T.U.C. now asked the Government for an assurance that the Trade Disputes Act of 1927 would be amended, Chamberlain indicated that trade unions were on probation for the

course of the war and hinted that their behaviour would influence the Government's attitude on legislation.

So it was only when Winston Churchill took over the premiership from Chamberlain in May, 1940, and promptly invited Ernest Bevin to become Minister of Labour, that the T.U.C. won its fight, not only to be heard by government, but to participate in it. At last, the men outside were *in*; and in to stay.

Nevertheless, during the bleak decade in which the T.U.C. had been held at arms length by Governments it had done a colossal amount of work. So much so that when war broke out a unique portfolio had been compiled of detailed policies for advancing the nation's welfare.

During the 1930's, also, the T.U.C. had continued to exercise vigilance about, and to react towards, any Government policy or action that could be of concern to working people and their families. And it had attempted itself to sponsor legislation that would be of benefit to them.

However, the sponsoring process proved difficult—much more difficult in this decade than it had been earlier, when M.P.s of the new-born Labour Party had been able to work on Asquith's Liberal Government with very fruitful results. But the Parliamentary Labour Party Opposition of the 1930's was in a weak position and attempts to introduce legislation either through the Parliamentary Party or through Private Members' Bills inevitably failed.

A melancholy case in point was the fate of the Workmen's Compensation Bill, a complete draft of which had been prepared by the T.U.C.'s Social Insurance Department that had been set up in 1928 at the time of the move to Transport House. This Bill sought compulsory insurance by employers to cover risks to their employees, so that injured workers and persons suffering from diseases contracted at work would be properly provided for. The Bill was presented to Parliament as a Private Member's Bill on several occasions in the 1930's, but it never reached the statute book so a major reform of the law on workmen's compensation had to await the election of the Labour Government and the Industrial Injuries Act of 1946.

Thus the General Council were obliged to look increasingly towards the Govern-

ment of the day—notwithstanding the fact that it was a Conservative Government—for sponsoring legislation beneficial to workpeople. This approach, however, met with only occasional success. For example, after consistent pressure for legislation to protect young people and women at work, the Government eventually introduced the 1937 Factories Act and many clauses were altered after representations from the T.U.C. Nevertheless, despite the success of this particular exercise in *ad hoc* consultation, permanent machinery for consistent consultation with the T.U.C. had to await the outbreak of the second world war.

But, if in the decade before the war, consultation was only fitful, actual T.U.C. and union participation in the official committees—responsible for advising on the administration of the gradually growing Government agencies and services—was increasing steadily, if slowly; from participation in a mere two at the beginning of the 1930's to ten by the end of 1939. So it was clear that the development of a number of T.U.C. departments, staffed with specialists, to service its members serving on these official committees, was beginning to prove itself.

These specialist departments also serviced the T.U.C.'s own committees; and thereby enabled the T.U.C. to take the initiative in formulating some extremely comprehensive policies on the control of industry. Public ownership (which was only one of the means of state control over industry advocated by the T.U.C.) was argued in terms of Ministerial responsibility through public corporations (see pages 100 and 101). Workers' directors, whatever their trade union connections, were not to be appointed, or to act, as trade union *representatives*. The T.U.C. looked for union participation in the future socialised or publicly controlled industries through the development of traditional collective bargaining and the extension of joint consultation. This line of thinking ran parallel with that which had begun to prevail in the Labour Party, after 1931, under Herbert Morrison's influence.

These detailed plans were for the future. Meanwhile, in the dismal present of the 1930's when British industry was ailing and the world was going down the long slide towards war, the T.U.C. concentrated much of its effort and resources on changing the nation's opinions. This was attempted through comprehensive memoranda—usually backed up by oral evidence and most frequently underpinned by a member of the General Council serving on the body which was carrying out a given investigation—to a great number of Royal Commissions, Committees of Inquiry and Departmental Committees.

One of the T.U.C.'s principal concerns at this time was to educate the nation (and, if possible, the Government) about education. The 1930's were a period in which today's commonplace orthodoxies about "child-centred" primary education were generally considered to be eccentric, or, at best, impracticable. The T.U.C. utterly rejected that defeatist notion.

As for secondary education, the principle of secondary education for all (which was eventually to be enshrined in the Education Act of 1944) had been theoretically accepted in the 1920's.

For the trade union Movement, secondary education in practice meant the abolition of fees, a minimum school-leaving age of 16, and a common form of provision of "multi-lateral" (later called "comprehensive") schools for all children. The T.U.C. recognised, earlier than most, that second-class secondary moderns could not provide educational equality for the persistently underprivileged children of working people. And it said as much to the Spens Committee, which reported in 1938. But it was not until the 1960's that the T.U.C.'s radical reforming policies of the 1930's were widely accepted by public opinion, and acted on by governments.

On the economic front, this period saw the theories of John Maynard Keynes provide the sound intellectual framework for the views which trade unionists had always instinctively held and known to be right. Some of those were reflected in the T.U.C.'s policies on fiscal and monetary matters, and also in its attitude to certain industrial problems, such as that of the "Special Areas". All these questions were the subject of major inquiries by the State; and to most of the inquiries the T.U.C. submitted evidence and conclusions.

For example, to the Macmillan Committee on Finance and Industry, on which J. M. Keynes and an extremely receptive Ernest Bevin both served, the T.U.C. submitted evidence which included the following two important paragraphs:

". . . it seems clear that many disputes are caused by the readjustment of the wage level, up or down, as prices fluctuate. Consequently it would seem that if stability of the level of prices could be obtained, there would be a diminution of industrial disputes . . . Stability of prices averts this difficulty and wage adjustments can then be based on other considerations such as productivity and the state of trade.

"We are certainly of the opinion that this policy [the return to the Gold Standard] was largely responsible for the coal dispute and the National Strike in 1926. It is a matter for profound regret that the Government entered upon this policy without consultation with organised labour. In view of the close connection between the monetary factor and industrial conditions, we hold the view very strongly that decisions of this kind, which inevitably affect industry, should not be taken without consultation with the Trade Union Movement."

But it was not only the T.U.C.'s thinking that was tinged by Keynsian theories. Keynes's work was not without influence in the policies and expedients of the National Government itself.

"Keynes" as G. D. H. Cole wrote, "could not . . . prevent the old notions being acted on when the slump hit Great Britain in 1931. But even under the 'National' Government it was no longer possible for deflation to be carried to the extreme . . .

"It was not admitted that the Government had a responsibility for maintaining either wages or employment; but up to a point they were maintained because no-one in authority dared push the attack on them to the extremes to which it would have been pushed before Trade Unions had become a power and before the 'New Economics' had at any rate shaken a great many persons' confidence in the 'Old'."

The concern of the General Council of the T.U.C. for the adequacy of its case, no matter what the subject in hand might be, and its consequential concern for a public hearing and for influence on the country's affairs, is perhaps most clearly to be discerned in the methods that were used for the purpose of co-operating with the medical profession and the nation's scientists.

A Joint Committee of the British Medical Association and the T.U.C., set up in 1938 with Dr. Charles Hill and

J. L. Smyth (of the T.U.C. Social Insurance Department) as joint secretaries, immediately got down to tackling two major problems: the problem of how best to establish a National Maternity Service, and the problem of how best to meet the need for Rehabilitation Centres for men and women injured in industrial accidents.

The news that the General Council of the T.U.C. had decided to establish a Scientific Advisory Committee to enable Congress and its constituent unions to secure the consultative help and advice of leading scientists in some systematic and regular way, was announced by Ernest Bevin in his Presidential Address to the 1937 Congress.

Early in 1938, the British Association for the Advancement of Science requested that it should be allowed to nominate the members of the Advisory Council's Committee, so as to ensure political independence and scientific disinterestedness. Among the distinguished scientists subsequently nominated were Sir John Boyd Orr and Sir Daniel Hall (Nutrition and Agriculture); Professor P. M. S. Blackett (Physics); Professor Lancelot Hogben (Population); and Professor J. D. Bernal (Metallurgy).

In July, 1939, the Advisory Committee set out a list of matters about which it felt that consultation was desirable. These included: researches into industrial fatigue, strain, shorter working hours; nutrition and standard of living; industrial population distribution; effects of technological changes; new uses for coal and other minerals; the organisation, use and distribution of power; smoke, dust and noise abatement; and current research in relation to industrial and occupational diseases with a view to their prevention.

So, in a number of ways, the T.U.C. by the end of the 1930's had accumulated information and constructive views on a wide range of subjects, about which it might well feel that it had a right to be heard by governments. In fact, by the outbreak of war there was no other major institution—not excluding the political parties—that was in possession of such comprehensive and detailed policies for advancing the nation's welfare as the T.U.C. An asset for which the post-war Labour Government was destined to be truly thankful.   ■

# In the wake of the general strike . . . the TUC examines trade union structure

*A. J. Cook, fiery leader of the miners union, which after the collapse of the General Strike on May 12, stayed out until the end of November.*

*Demonstration along the Embankment, London, against the Trade Disputes and Trade Unions Bill, 1927; part of a massive campaign organised by the T.U.C. throughout the country.*

BEVIN AND CITRINE now persistently emphasised the essential purpose of trade unionism: to safeguard and improve the standards of working people within the prevailing social system, and whatever government might be in power —though without abandoning trade union support for the political labour Movement.

To this end, they demanded recognition of the *right* of the trade union Movement to be consulted by Government and employers about *any* matter affecting workers' living standards or working conditions. And they also concerned themselves, as a priority, with everything which had a bearing on the efficiency of trade unions and the trade union Movement. Citrine, in particular, had a genius for tackling problems of organisation, structure and administration. It was he who rationalised the T.U.C. office, developed the T.U.C. Research Department, and, with Bevin, promoted the expansion of education especially through scholarships to Ruskin College, Oxford.

Citrine also played a major part in the General Council's inquiry into the structure of the trade union Movement, requested by the 1924 Congress at Hull, and the results of which were presented

The two dominant personalities in this new phase of T.U.C. history: Ernest Bevin and Walter Citrine.

by the General Council in a report to the 1927 Congress. In the interim, Citrine had written a crucial memorandum on the question of structure.

"I pointed out", he writes in his autobiography, "that the Trades Union Congress was itself a federal organization. I emphasised that it could not lay down any plan of reorganization which its affiliated unions could be compelled to accept. No matter what the T.U.C. said, the individual unions always had the last word. . . .

"I set out to examine the objects of trade unionism as stated in their rule books, but whilst the majority of the unions had been established with the primary purpose of dealing with improvements in wages and working conditions, in only a small number of cases was there a clear recognition that the trade union Movement had any wider purpose. 'Function must determine structure', I wrote, 'and that type of organization which will suit the minimum needs of a union's own members will not necessarily be best for the attainment of all the broader objects.' I defined these objects as (1) improvement of wages and working conditions, (2) a measure of control of industry, and

(3) the ability to defend the workers against any onslaught by capitalism. . . .

"As to the defects in trade union structure, they had long been apparent. I set them out as (1) sectionalism, (2) competition for members, (3) unions offering different rates of contributions and benefits for apparently the same services, (4) demarcation of work, and (5) lack of a co-ordinated policy."

Citrine's thinking was clearly discernible in the General Council's Report on Trade Union Structure to the 1927 Congress. The original Hull Congress resolution of 1924 had called on the General Council to draw up a scheme for union organisation by industry. The General Council's 1927 Report argued that industrial unions were not practicable. Instead, it proposed a number of major developments, such as the grouping of craft and occupational unions so as to reduce sectional conflicts and demarcation disputes; the setting-up of joint bodies of unions, with power to deal with negotiations and trade matters —but without interfering with union autonomy on administrative and domestic matters; and the establishment of a common fund for the trade benefits of such joint bodies.

Closer co-ordination of policies on matters of general concern to the Movement was also called for by the General Council. They stressed the necessity for centralised negotiations with the Confederation of Employers Organisations to deal with general questions for the whole Movement, and recommended that "this necessary co-ordination should be in the hands of the T.U.C. through the medium of the General Council". Though it was to be some 40 years before this idea came at all close to getting off the ground. The General Council had much more success, however, when it came to seeking authority to deal with union disputes. By 1924 a number of "main principles" of good trade union practice had been established and formed the terms of reference of the T.U.C. Disputes Committee when considering union disputes over membership.

The experience gained in dealing with a number of disputes in the late 20's and 30's led the General Council to make further proposals to the 1939 Bridlington Congress and these were approved. These "Bridlington principles" form the basis on which the T.U.C. adjudicates on disputes about membership to this day.

## TUC ballots the miners
## to defeat company unionism

*A unique incident in the history of the T.U.C. came in 1928 when the T.U.C. organised a ballot in the Notts coal field to discover whether a newly formed company union had the support of mineworkers. After an extensive publicity campaign by the T.U.C. under the banner "Vote for real trade unionism" the miners voted solidly 9 to 1 in favour of the old established and independent Nottinghamshire Miners Association.*

*Transport House, opened by Ramsay MacDonald in the summer of 1928.*

"MAY, 1928" wrote Alan Bullock in his book, 'The Life and Times of Ernest Bevin', "saw the realisation of another of Bevin's dreams, the opening of Transport House. To the passer-by, cutting across Smith Square and turning a curious eye towards the bombed ruins of the eighteenth-century church of St. John, Transport House is a large, not very distinguished brick building at the corner of Dean Bradley Street. Bevin saw it with different eyes. He remembered the shabby terrace house in Princes Street, Bristol, where he had joined the Dockers' Union; to him it was nothing short of marvellous that a working men's organisation, with a subscription of 6d. a week, could rise from renting a house in a back street to building, at a cost of well over £50,000, an eight-storey office building of its own, within a stone's throw of the House of Lords.

"It was a triumph which even the most disgruntled of his critics would find it hard to grudge him, for if ever a building was due to the determination of one man, it was Transport House. Since his visit to America in 1915, Bevin had had in his mind a headquarters equal to the status which he claimed for the trade union movement. No other union in the country up to that time had built offices of anything like the size or spaciousness of Transport House, which was designed to house the national offices, not only of the Transport and General Workers' Union but of the Trades Union Congress and the Labour Party as well. He had the imagination to grasp the psychological as well as the practical advantage to the Movement of an impressive building of its own with the political and trade union sides brought together under the single roof . . ."

Ben Turner, a leader of the wool textile workers, was chairman of the General Council of the Trades Union Congress in 1928. Ever since the end of the General Strike, the General Council had been considering whether it might not now be desirable to establish some machinery for joint consultation about the more general problems of industry between the representative employers' organisations and the representatives of the trade unions.

Hints, inspired by Citrine, and developed by George Hicks at the 1927 Congress, met with no response from the F.B.I. and the National Confederation of Employers' Organisations. But, shortly afterwards, the General Council received a constructive letter signed jointly by Sir Alfred Mond and a number of other eminent industrialists.

Sir Alfred Mond, Chairman of Imperial Chemical Industries. His letter to the General Council extended an invitation to a conference at which the whole field of industrial reorganisation and industrial relations could be reviewed. "We realise", he wrote, "that industrial reorganisation can only be undertaken with the co-operation of those empowered to speak for organised labour. . . We believe that the common interests which bind us are more powerful than the apparently divergent interests that separate."

At the first session of the "Mond-Turner Talks"—as they came to be called—Mond indicated the kind of thing that he and his fellow employers would like to discuss. The proposed subjects included rationalisation and amalgamation; housing, health and unemployment insurance; education and industry; works councils; security and status of the workers; financial participation by the workers; investigation into the causes of disputes; and the creation of a permanent standing committee.

"Mondism" was soon denounced by the Communists as a flagrant example of class collaboration. It was also attacked, unavailingly, at the 1928 Trades Union Congress by A. J. Cook. No concrete results stemmed from the Mond-Turner talks; but the experience of them influenced the thinking of T.U.C. leaders for years to come.

*Walter Citrine, in 1928, as President of the International Federation of Trade Unions—a post which he filled for many years. And (left) Citrine, with Leon Jouhaux of France, and C. Mertens, of Belgium, at the International Congress in London in July, 1936, when Hitler was already on the move.*

## Citrine and the IFTU

The I.F.T.U. had developed out of the International Secretariat of Trade Union Centres, in 1913. In the mid '20s the General Council of the T.U.C. used its influence to try and

# 1929: Labour Government back in office

*The new look of the "flapper vote", which had been bestowed on women of 21 by Stanley Baldwin's Government. After the May, 1929, general election—which returned only 261 Conservative M.P.s, as against 288 Labour and 57 Liberal Members —many Tories grumbled that Baldwin should never have gone and given the vote to all those girls.*

arrange for the smooth enrolment of the Russian trade union Movement into the I.F.T.U. But the other continental unions were suspicious of Russian motives. The Russians themselves did little to abate those suspicions. And the project lapsed.

In 1931, the offices of the I.F.T.U. were moved from their original location in Amsterdam to Berlin. Two years later, the Nazis came to power, and proceeded to suppress the German trade union Movement. In the same year the General Council of the T.U.C. drafted a report on "Dictatorship and the Trade Union Movement", underlining the lessons of the German Movement's experience since the Treaty of Versailles. This report was overwhelmingly approved by the Brighton Congress of 1933.

*Some of the voters who, in this era of chronic and increasing unemployment, sent Labour back to Westminster as the largest single party in the Commons.*

# As the unemployment figures soar towards the three million mark the TUC solidly opposes the MacDonald-Snowden 'economies'

EVER SINCE Britain went back to the Gold Standard in 1925 more than a million and a quarter workers had been unemployed: a fact of which the voters in the 1929 general election evidently took note. So the new Labour Government decided to set up a Committee on Finance and Industry, whose President was Lord Macmillan, a judge, and whose only trade unionist member was Ernest Bevin. The Committee was required to inquire into banking, finance and credit, and into the effect of monetary policy upon employment and trade.

To this Committee the Trades Union Congress submitted evidence which indicated that the deflationary situation caused by the return to the Gold Standard had been accentuated by a whole series of wage cuts. At the same time the employers were arguing for cuts in the wages of public employees, cuts in expenditure on the social services and cuts in unemployment benefit, as a means of keeping the country on the Gold Standard and safeguarding the pound. These were arguments of a kind to which—by July, 1931, when the number of unemployed had risen to 2,750,000—Philip Snowden, the Labour Chancellor, was inclined to lend an ear.

His inclinations were powerfully reinforced by the report of Sir George May's Committee on National Expenditure, which Snowden himself had set up early in 1931, at the behest of the Parliamentary Liberal Party. On August 1st it came out with recommendations for the wholesale slashing of government expenditure.

This method of "solving" the economic crisis was directly contrary to the thinking of the T.U.C. and of the General Council's Economic Committee, which had been created in 1929. Bevin, who had learnt a great deal from J. M. Keynes during sessions of the Macmillan Committee about the economic consequences of deflation and the potentialities of expansion, was able to kindle the imagination of members of the General Council's Economic Committee with his own enthusiasm for some of Keynes's expansionist policies. And, early in 1931, the General Council of the T.U.C. issued a document which stressed the necessity of maintaining at all costs the purchasing power of consumers.

But, by this time, Snowden and MacDonald had their ears cocked in

*From the Gold Standard to the Slag Standard: the face of unemployment in the 1930's.*

quite another direction—the direction of the City and its exponents of "sound finance". By mid-August they had evidently made up their minds that there was no alternative to adopting most of the May Committee's recommendations, whatever the T.U.C. might think. However, MacDonald and Snowden were eventually persuaded by Arthur Henderson to call, on August 20th, a meeting of the T.U.C. General Council, the Cabinet Economy Committee and various other members of the Labour Party Executive, to review the financial crisis.

At this meeting at Transport House MacDonald and Snowden argued that, if the drain on gold were to be stopped and the budget balanced, there would have to be drastic cuts in government expenditure—including teachers' salaries, Servicemen's and policemen's pay —and severe economies in the national insurance system; as well as increased taxation of an undisclosed kind.

The T.U.C. representatives listened to these arguments, and then retired to discuss them. They decided to oppose any of the Government's proposals

which could make still worse the already appalling situation of the nearly three million unemployed. They also agreed to put forward their own counter-proposals: for a graduated levy on all sections of the community; for a tax on all fixed-interest-bearing securities, which had become worth more as prices had fallen; and for the temporary suspension of the Sinking Fund.

When Citrine and Bevin led a five-man T.U.C. delegation to Downing Street that same evening, Snowden noted that the General Council appeared to be opposed to all the Government's recommended economies, without the implementation of which, he claimed, the number of unemployed might well rise to ten million.

Next day, Henderson and several other Cabinet Ministers, emboldened by the T.U.C. General Council's attitude, stiffened their own opposition to the Macdonald-Snowden plan.

On August 23rd, MacDonald thought it expedient to resign. As he had expected, he was asked to carry on, regardless—this time, as head of a "National" Government.

# October 1931: by playing fast and loose with the word 'national', MacDonald's coalition government gets itself returned to power with a massive majority

*In early September, 1931, one week after he and his handful of supporters have been expelled from the Labour Party, an uneasy Ramsay MacDonald meets the Press in his Seaham Harbour constituency. During the previous month Citrine and Bevin and the whole of the T.U.C. have been concerned, equally with the Parliamentary Labour Party, to ensure that the repercussions upon the labour Movement of the MacDonaldites' defection shall be as small as possible.*

## The kind of thing that the electors were told . . .

**WE MUST THINK OF OUR SAVINGS AND OUR HOME. THAT'S WHY I'M VOTING FOR THE NATIONAL GOVERNMENT**

*It's just common sense!*

**VOTE NATIONAL LABOUR**

*Smokeless Chimneys and—* **ANXIOUS MOTHERS!**

**THE REMEDY** VOTE FOR THE **NATIONAL GOVERNMENT**

*Vote National! Vote Conservative! Vote National Labour! Vote National Liberal! Whatever you do, vote anti-Socialist. Because, if you let the Socialists in, they will pillage your savings in the Post Office Savings Bank—as Mr. Philip Snowden*

*said in his B.B.C. broadcast. And Mr. Snowden has been a Socialist himself: he should know.*
*But the return to Parliament of 417 Conservatives, plus an assortment of Liberals and National Labourites—as*

*against only 49 Labour Party M.P.s— did not turn out to be the remedy. Not for the country. Not for the pound, which was given a speedy divorce from the Gold Standard. And least of all for the unemployed.*

# The thirties

*Just a part of the massive crowd which gathered in Hyde Park on February 5, 1933, to protest against mounting unemployment and the Government's measures for dealing with it. The General Council's Report for the year saw it as "One of the largest gatherings ever held in this history of the Movement".*

THROUGHOUT their terms of office during the 1930's, neither the National Government nor the Conservative Government had given any indication that they were capable of finding any solution to the unemployment problem. Indeed, until war came, no solution was found. Even as late as the autumn of 1939, three years after the Jarrow marchers had brought home just what it meant to be out of work without hope, Wigan, where the picture on the left was taken, was still left with 10 of its 40 pits idle. In a town of 85,000 people, some 9,500 employable men and women—11 per cent—were out of work. But for the war, and its demands for manpower and womanpower, they would probably have remained so.

The General Council, powerless though they were to implant Keynes's ideas in the minds that made the vital decisions, vigorously used the time-honoured methods of mass meetings as well as trying in talks with Government to get top level action on the unemployment problem.

Early in 1933 they organised a massive national demonstration on unemployment in 21 major cities up and down the country and in London's Hyde Park. However, their main task in these years was to convince the Government that it was responsible for the level of economic activity in the country. In July 1939, for example, the General Council met the Prime Minister—after a decade of

unparalleled unemployment—to argue the case for a National Planning Board which would have the continuing function of "making a careful and detailed investigation of the unemployment situation in all its aspects, and of drawing up and submitting proposals for dealing with the situation as revealed by its investigations". The Prime Minister accepted that there might be a case for a purely advisory body—indeed, it had been in his mind for some time, but the reason he had not yet put it into effect "was due to very heavy pressure of other business". He hoped the meeting with the deputation would serve to remind him of the importance of the matter.

# The state of industry and TUC plans for its control

*On the stocks at Clydebank, liner 534 lies half completed—deserted because of the depression. Later she was to become the most luxurious liner in the world—the Queen Mary.*

AFTER the shattering defeat of the political wing of the labour Movement in the 1931 election, Citrine took steps to secure representation for the T.U.C. General Council in the co-ordinating body known as the National Joint Council, equal to that of the Labour Party National Executive and the Parliamentary Labour Party combined; and he affirmed the right of the General Council to "initiate and participate in any political matter which it deems to be of direct concern to its constituents." (As a result of the Bevin-inspired reorganisation and redevelopment of the "Daily Herald", the T.U.C. was already entitled to nominate four out of the nine directors of Labour's only national newspaper.)

Citrine also initiated and guided the General Council's Report on Trade Unions and the Control of Industry, which was presented to the 1932 Congress at Newcastle. This general report, and the succession of particular policy statements which in due course stemmed from it, did much of the spadework for any future Labour Government which might be looking for a blue-print for socialisation or other forms of public control.

The report itself examined the various reasons for which it would be desirable to bring an industry or service under public control; the various methods by which such control could be exercised; and the alternative ways of compensating former shareholders.

At the 1932 Congress, the report was well received—except for the section dealing with the representation of the trade unions on the controlling bodies or Boards of the socialised industries.

This section suggested "that members of such a Board should in all cases be appointed by the Government, and should consist neither of technical experts nor of representatives of particular interests, but of persons appointed solely for their ability to fill the position. Any of the persons appointed might be chosen from the business world, the Trade Union Movement, the financial world, public administration and so on, but not as representatives of such sectional interests".

A final decision was deferred until the Brighton Congress of 1933. Meanwhile, answers to a questionnaire circulated to affiliated trade unions showed a majority in favour of the trade unions having the right to nominate persons for appointment to the controlling Boards of socialised undertakings.

After discussion between a committee of the General Council and a committee of the Labour Party executive, a joint statement was drawn up for submission to Congress and to the Labour Party Conference.

The statement read in part:

". . . In the first place we think it desirable to point out the distinction between the various functions of management and control. A considerable part of the activities of industrial managements at present is concerned with the settlement of wages, hours, and all the other working conditions that most nearly affect the workers day by day. These matters are at present adjusted by negotiation between employers and Trade Unions. In our view, this method must continue to apply in the case of socialised undertakings. The adjustment of wages and working conditions

*A strike of Lancashire cotton operatives, in August 1932. The Trades Union Congress of the same year receives from the General Council a long report on the public control and regulation of industry. Following this, the T.U.C. publishes at intervals a series of detailed major statements on the public control of specific industries: in 1934, a statement on the*

*socialisation of steel: in 1935, a statement on the public control of the cotton industry where the amalgamated weavers lost half their members between 1926 and 1939; in 1936, statements on the socialisation of coal, and the public control of electricity distribution.*

must be undertaken by direct negotiations between the Trade Unions and the Managements of these concerns, and Trade Union rights, including the right to strike, must be fully maintained.

"Then there is the day-to-day administration of the concern. This is quickly becoming a profession, and the persons undertaking this work will have to be trained as business administrators.

"Over and above the day-to-day administration there must necessarily be a Board of Management and Control, and this Board must consist of competent and suitable persons. Organised Labour claims for Trade Unions in the industry the right to nominate persons for appointment to such a Board. This claim of Organised Labour that it shall have its place in the control and direction of publicly-owned industries is accepted.

"It is agreed that in order to give effect to this object there shall be consultation between the responsible Minister and the Trade Unions concerned."

At the Brighton Congress of 1933, this joint statement was adopted.

*During the first weeks of National Government rule, 20,000 civil servants, with 20 bands, march from the Thames Embankment to Hyde Park, to protest against wage and salary cuts.*

*Among the industries where trade unions were making their strongest headway despite high unemployment figures nationally were the expanding motor industry where production line techniques were now in common use, and the fast growing aircraft industry which was adding to the demand for both traditional and new engineering skills.*

THE LARGE-SCALE unemployment which disfigured the face of Britain during the decade before the second world war did not prevent a substantial increase in trade union membership throughout a large number of industries.

The development of mass-production consumer industries such as the clothing industry, and comparatively new industries such as the aircraft industry, as well as the expansion of services such as transport, and distribution where semi-skilled and female labour abounded, were major factors in the growth of many unions.

During the inter-war period, membership was doubled in the Tailors and Garment Workers Union; in the Electrical Trades Union and the Amalgamated Engineering Union; in the two main unions in the distributive trades, and in the Transport and General Workers Union which, in 1937, overtook the Miners' Federation, and, with a membership of over 650,000, became the largest trade union in the world. A similar growth in union membership was also adding to the strength of the

National Union of General and Municipal Workers.

Yet this expansion was not without problems. Many, as Henry Pelling wrote in "A History of British Trade Unionism", "were caused by the fact that the expansion largely took place in parts of the country where unionism had previously been weak or non-existent. . . . Other problems arose from the fact that in comparatively new industries, such as motor manufacture, there were serious demarcation conflicts between different unions, especially skilled unions, and there was little prospect of the emergence of a single bargaining agency for the whole industry. The unions, short of funds as they often were after the depression, were slow to take advantage of the opportunities in the new areas, and often it was a rank-and-file movement, not infrequently led by Communists, which led to the 'capture' of new factories in the London suburbs, at Oxford, and elsewhere."

The growth and spread of trade

unionism inevitably involved disputes and struggles for union recognition; and, in support of those struggles, strikes—which were often led by shop stewards without the authority of the union.

In his "Post-War History of the British Working Class", A. Hutt has given details of a number of these strikes: starting, way back in 1929, with the ten weeks' strike of girl workers in the Rego clothing factory in London for union recognition, and with the strike of 8,000 men—three-quarters of whom were unorganised—at the Austin motor works, against piece-work changes and regrading. The clothing industry in 1933-4 produced two more successful strikes for union recognition, at Coleman's Mantle Factory and at Fairdale's.

At this time the aggressive use of the stop watch to time jobs as a means of speeding up production provoked a crop of strikes, including ones at the Lucas Motor Accessories Works in Birmingham, at the Venesta Plywood Factory in East London, at Hope's Steel Window

# Young workers
# fight for a fair chance

AT A TIME when many of today's well-established industries were just beginning to make their mark on the industrial scene, young workers were making a similar impact through the unions and the T.U.C.

In the later years of the decade a number of strikes of apprentices took place in the engineering industry and as a result the Amalgamated Engineering Union took the affairs of young workers out of the hands of the master to whom they were indentured by gaining negotiating rights for them with employers.

The T.U.C. at this time was on a similar tack. In 1937 the General Council successfully put a number of amendments to the Factories Bill before it got to the House of Commons which led to the working hours of the 14-16 age group—and women—being reduced by

eight hours to 40 a week. In the same year a Congress resolution prompted the General Council to draw up a "Youth Charter" which was put to the Trades Union Congress at Blackpool a year later.

The first man to speak on it was aptly suited to do so. He was a 20-year-old delegate who alone represented his union—the wheelwrights and coach-makers. He stressed that the youth of Britain "must not enrol under the banner of fascism as they do in Italy and Germany".

The Charter called for minimum wage rates, a 40-hour week, annual holidays, abolition of overtime and night work for workers under 18, adequate insurance benefits for young workers without a means test, and time off for technical training.

*Young apprentices from Glasgow's shipbuilding and engineering industries out on strike in April, 1937.*

Works in Birmingham, and the Firestone Tyre Factory in Brentford.

Though many were unofficial, they normally resulted in substantial increases in union membership.

In 1935 there were more successful strikes for union recognition by provincial busmen and by workers in the Hawker Aircraft factories. In the following year, other aircraft concerns, such as de Havilland, Fairey, Handley Page and Parnall were affected by strikes which often centred on the recognition of shop stewards. And in December 1936 a national delegate conference convened by the Amalgamated Engineering Union resolved to press a claim for a national aircraft agreement, with wage increases.

And so, by 1938, not only had many individual unions made notable advances in membership, but overall membership of the trade union movement, which had fallen away in the slump which followed the General Strike, had now begun to climb once more—to the six million mark, and beyond.

*Off to the Imperial Economic Conference held at Ottawa in July, 1932, go Stanley Baldwin, J. H. Thomas, Neville Chamberlain, and other representatives of Britain's National Government. This Government now sets a precedent by inviting the Trades Union Congress to send two representatives to the Ottawa Conference, to advise on industrial matters. The representatives chosen by the T.U.C. are John Bromley, of the locomotive men, who was the current chairman of the T.U.C.'s Economic Committee, and Walter Citrine.*

# The TUC and the British Commonwealth

DURING the late 1920's and throughout the 1930's, the T.U.C. became increasingly concerned with the conditions of life and work in other countries of the Commonwealth. The first straw in the wind was a meeting at the I.L.O. Conference in 1927, of the workers' representatives from Great Britain, India, Canada, New Zealand and the Irish Free State. In the following year a conference was convened in London for representatives of the trade union movements of Australia, Canada, Ceylon, Great Britain, India, Ireland, Palestine, South Africa and Trinidad. The subjects examined by the Conference included: racial problems and governments; trading in the Commonwealth; and social insurance schemes.

These Conferences have been held from time to time ever since 1927. The concern for conditions in Commonwealth countries began to take practical shape when the second Labour Government appointed a Colonial Development Advisory Committee. The task of this Committee, of which Ernest Bevin was a member, was to advise on applications from the colonies for grants, under the Colonial Development Fund Act of 1929, to assist specific schemes of development, such as the Zambesi Bridge project.

"It was the first time Bevin came into contact with the struggling impoverished world of the under-developed countries", wrote Alan Bullock. "It aroused an interest and a sympathy in him which he was never to lose, and which bore fruit in the support he gave to Arthur Creech-Jones as Colonial Secretary of the post-war Labour Government, and in the Colombo Plan, the last great project to which he put his hand at the very end of his life".

In 1930, the T.U.C. and the Federation of British Industries, assuming not unreasonably that the Imperial Conference of that year would be used partly for a discussion of economic matters, issued a joint statement urging the creation of permanent machinery for economic consultation between the various nations of the Commonwealth. But as, in the event, it was impossible fully to consider economic subjects at the 1930 Imperial Conference, agreement was reached to proceed with a special Imperial Economic Conference at Ottawa in July, 1932. To this conference the British Government invited the T.U.C. to send two representatives.

The T.U.C. and the F.B.I. again issued a joint statement, this time pointing the need for co-operation between both sides of industry, and echoing the consensus of the Mond-Turner talks.

The T.U.C. itself had already been moving away from Free Trade doctrine, and had been recognising the need for trading policies that gave a degree of stability to the prices of primary products, so as to ensure some stable markets for British manufactured goods.

Later, in 1937, the T.U.C. set up its own Colonial Advisory Committee to investigate the conditions in which peoples of the Commonwealth lived and worked; and to see how far the T.U.C. might be able to contribute towards improving those conditions and raising the peoples' standards of life.

This Committee, which still exists under the name Commonwealth Advisory Committee, eventually succeeded in persuading the Colonial Office under Malcolm MacDonald to set up a Labour Department, advised by a Committee on which the T.U.C. was represented.

In 1938, the importance of the T.U.C.'s constructive concern with colonial conditions was further recognised by the British Government, when Walter Citrine was appointed a member of the Royal Commission that was instructed to investigate social and economic conditions in the West Indies, where serious riots had been taking place.

*Autumn, 1932. On the eve of his coming to power, Adolf Hitler swears Nazi Members of the Reichstag to allegiance.*

# The twilight of the German trade unions

OF THE MELANCHOLY situation in Germany in early February 1933, just after Hitler became Chancellor, Citrine wrote in his autobiography:—"In the next session of our International Federation of Trade Unions meeting we discussed the removal of our office from Germany. We were reluctant to do this, as it might appear to the German trade unionists that we were deserting them. I said I hesitated to comment on the situation, which seemed to me to be growing alarming. It was almost a repetition of what happened in Italy in the early stages of fascist dictatorship. Hitler had already established a censorship of the Press. He had mobilised the radio for party propaganda. It might be that at the forthcoming elections the people would be intimidated by the Nazis.

"I asked what our German comrades thought about the situation. Leipart, who was the leader of the German trade unions, made a statement suggesting that the trade unions in the various countries should exert public pressure through the Press, emphasising that freedom of action had practically ceased in Germany. He blamed the communists for splitting the ranks of the trade unions. All that they were concerned with was creating a Soviet Germany. He assured us that all

arrangements had been made to meet any contingency and that the leaders only had to give the word. Then there would be a General Strike and that might lead to civil war".

None of what Leipart had envisaged actually happened.

The T.U.C. drafted a report on "Dictatorship and the Trade Union Movement" (previously mentioned) which underlined the lessons of the German trade unions' experience, and showed how the German communists' attacks on the unions and the social-democrats had weakened the whole labour Movement. Meanwhile—for the benefit of British communists and of those in the unions, the Labour Party and the I.L.P. who were advocating the idea of forming a United Front with them—the National Joint Council, representing both T.U.C. and Labour Party, published a manifesto which once more declared its opposition not only to fascism and Nazism, but also to communism.

In 1934, the General Council followed up this manifesto with what came to be described by the communists as the "Black Circular". This recommended all trade unions to exclude communists and fascists from responsible posts; and it laid down that any trades council

that wished to retain the formal recognition of Congress must exclude communist and fascist delegates.

*February, 1933. The Reichstag is set on fire; and German democracy goes up in smoke.*

*Dictator Mussolini's chosen opponents: the primitively armed troops of the Emperor of Abyssinia. "If you handed me Abyssinia on a silver plate" Mussolini was reported to have said, shortly before launching his invasion, "I would not accept it. For I am resolved to take it by force".*

# Collective security on trial: the TUC's attitude

THE IDEA of an international general strike to prevent governments going to war was advocated by the International Federation of Trade Unions when they met in 1933. Ernest Bevin thought this was nonsense, and told the Transport and General Workers Executive Council so. "Who and what is there to strike? Trade unionism has been destroyed in Italy and Germany; practically speaking, it does not exist in France; it is extremely weak in the U.S.A. . . . while there is no possibility of a general strike against the Russian government in the event of war. . .".

So, early in 1934, the General Council of the T.U.C. met the National Executive and the Parliamentary Com-

mittee of the Labour Party, and drafted a crucial statement which was called "War and Peace". The statement declared that it was the duty of the labour Movement "unflinchingly to support our Government in all the risks and consequences of fulfilling its duty to take part in collective action against a peace-breaker". And it warned forthrightly that there might be circumstances under which the Government "might have to use its military and naval forces in support of the League in restraining an aggressor nation".

The policy embodied in "War and Peace" was overwhelmingly endorsed by the 1934 Trades Union Congress at

Weymouth: near which town, exactly one hundred years earlier, the "Tolpuddle Martyrs" had administered their "illegal oaths", while founding a branch of the Friendly Society of Agricultural Labourers—and had been sentenced to transportation for daring so to do.

The centenary of the victimisation of the six Dorset labourers moved Ernest Bevin to a characteristic utterance. "Whenever I am asked about the dictatorship of the proletariat, of the Nazis", he exclaimed vehemently, "or any other form of it, I reply that I was born in a village and held under a dictatorship until I was fourteen—and I will see you to the devil before I have any more".

*Left to right, Sir Samuel Hoare and Pierre Laval, Foreign Ministers of Britain and France; and Anthony Eden, who replaced Hoare as Foreign Minister in December 1935, after the outraged protests from thousands of supporters of collective security which followed the proposal of the appeasing Hoare-Laval Pact.*

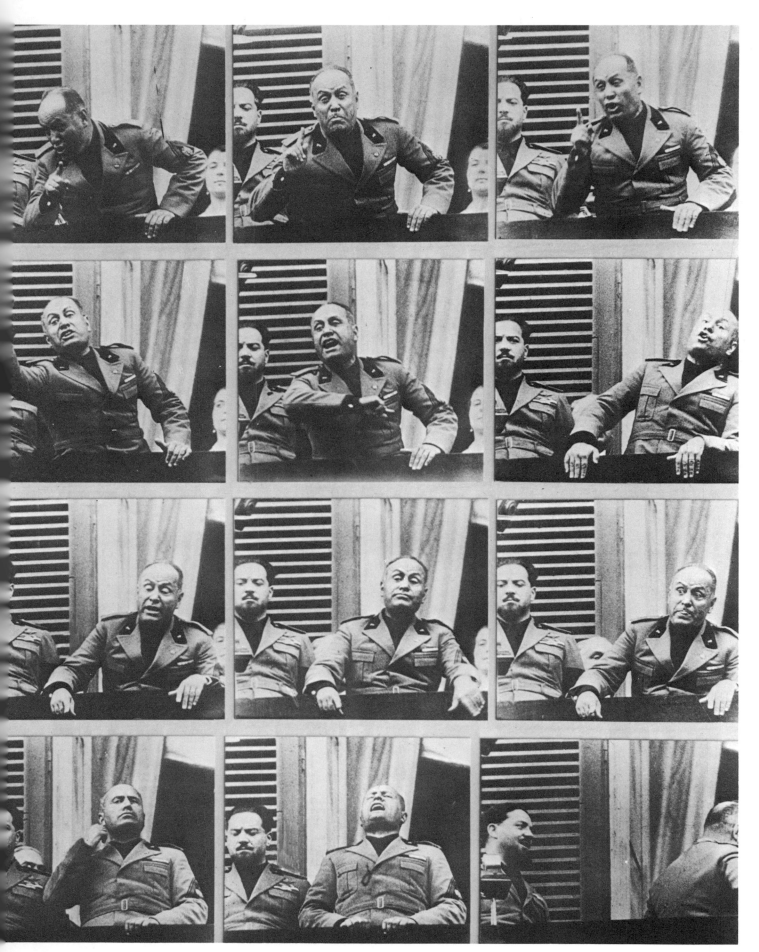

*One man who calculated, correctly, that League of Nations sanctions would never be fully enforced by governments against a war of aggression: Benito Mussolini in his prime.*

IN THE COURSE of moving a resolution in support of the League at the 1935 Trades Union Congress, Citrine declared: "There is only one way of dealing with a bully and that is by the use of force . . . It may mean war, but that is the thing we have to face. There is no real alternative now left to us but the applying of sanctions involving, in all possibility, war. But I say this. If we fail now, if we go back now, war is absolutely certain. I ask you what will happen to Germany, if Italy can treat with contempt the nations of the world who have plighted their word to preserve peace?"

*Fascists smashing windows of a Jewish tailor's shop in the Mile End Road in London's East End, scene of many pitched battles between the communists and fascists in the 1930's.*

# Inside the Labour Movement pacifist influence wanes

DURING 1935 the T.U.C. had become fully committed to the support of collective security, as the basis of its foreign policy line.

In May of the following year the National Council of Labour published a manifesto called "Labour and the Defence of Peace", which declared among other things that "Labour must be prepared to accept the consequences of its policy. A man who joins a trade union accepts the obligation of collective action in defence of its principles. A man who enjoys the collective security of a trade union must be prepared to take the risk of loyalty and his principles when a strike or lockout is threatened. Similarly, a Movement which supports the League system cannot desert it in a crisis".

So this was how matters now stood:— The labour Movement was committed to uphold the League Covenant and to support the use of military sanctions if required. But the League of Nations had no armed forces of its own. And the British labour Movement as a whole still hesitated to commit itself to the support of British re-armament under a British Government whose reluctance to use sanctions to the full against Italian aggression in Abyssinia had largely knocked the teeth out of the Covenant of the League of Nations.

When the Spanish war broke out in the middle of 1936, the British Government's obvious sympathy with General Franco and his rebels deepened the misgivings of those in the trade union and labour Movements who were dubious about helping a Conservative Government to re-arm.

But the T.U.C. had few reservations about the need for Britain's re-armament. In fact, Citrine's trip to the United States and Canada in 1934 had been made "specially for the purpose of bringing home to American trade unionists that, unless the aggressors were induced to abandon their designs, war on a world-wide scale was certain to break out". And there was clearly only one way, in Citrine's view, of inducing Mussolini and Hitler to call a halt.

# Fascism and Nazism find some admirers but overwhelming opposition in Britain

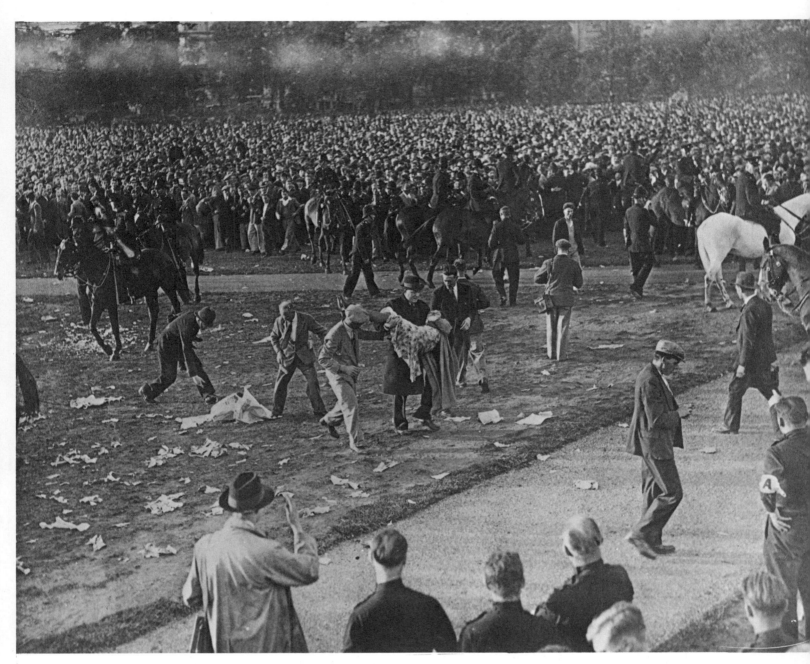

*Hyde Park, one of the favourite locations for fascist and anti-fascist demonstrations.*

*In 1933 the T.U.C. joined with the National Council of Labour in recommending a boycott of German goods. A message to trade unionists read "Our call for a ban on German goods and services is not designed to injure the German nation, but to bring home to their government that the crimes it has committed, and is still committing, will not be condoned by the peoples of the world."*

# The Spanish war, non-interventio

IN JULY, 1936, General Franco, backed by most of the Spanish Regular Army, launched a rebellion against the radical Republican Government of Spain, whose Prime Minister, Largo Caballero, had worked closely with Walter Citrine in the International Federation of Trade Unions. Two weeks after the revolt began, a joint meeting in Brussels of the I.F.T.U. and the Labour and Socialist International learned with surprise that Leon Blum, the Socialist Prime Minister of France, had declared against supplying arms to the Spanish Government, and was receiving support from other Powers including Great Britain for a policy of complete non-intervention, as being the policy most likely to prevent a European war.

It was this policy that the Trades Union Congress in September, despite sympathy for the Spanish Republicans and detestation of fascism, endorsed as the lesser evil, by 3 million votes to 50,000. But if the T.U.C. albeit reluctantly, fell into line with Leon Blum, Hitler and Mussolini did not. Non-intervention was not only not complete: it was

proving to be utterly one-sided. By the end of October the General Council joined with the Labour Party in demanding that the right to purchase arms should be restored to the Spanish Government. It was difficult, however, to see what could be done effectively to change the Government's non-intervention policy.

Citrine in his autobiography tells of this question being raised at a session of the General Council of the T.U.C. at Blackpool in September, 1938. He had asked unions who felt that the General Council's efforts to secure arms for the Spanish Government were inadequate and could be supplemented by some new policy, or action, to make specific suggestions as to how that could be done.

"In the Council's view" wrote Citrine "there were only two ways in which a reluctant Government's policy could be changed. One was by means of general propaganda in which the movement had been indulging vigorously, and the other was to take some kind of coercive action. It was clearly the latter course which was in the minds of those who

felt that the movement was not doing enough.

"I raised the issue of the justification for taking industrial action for a political objective. We were meeting at a time when contempt had been lavishly sprayed over Parliamentary institutions. It was said that democracy was played out and that government by consent, as distinct from dictatorship, was dead. I tried to show that it was not for the trade union Movement, which had repeatedly attested its belief in democracy, to strike a blow at its institutions. We ought not to give the fascists encouragement by ourselves trying to change by force the views of a democratically elected Parliament".

In the following year, the democratically elected Spanish Government was compelled to give up the unequal struggle against the combined Falangist, Italian fascist and Nazi armaments and forces. The massacre-bombing of Guernica had paid off; and the stage—and the pattern—was set for the second world war. The only thing now in doubt was the starting-date.

On the way to the Madrid front. An improvised citizen army, somewhat reinforced by volunteers from the western democracies serving in the International Brigade, goes out to grapple with the combined power of Franco's rebel regulars, fascist and Nazi troops and tanks and aircraft— and the British and French Governments' throttling non-intervention policy.

# nd the British labour Movement

Particularly after the outbreak of the Spanish Civil War in the summer of 1936, the deep division in Continental Europe between the fascist and the anti-fascist camps was reflected in the British political scene. Here Mosleyites protest against a union convoy of lorries loaded with food and medical supplies for Republican Spain.

Up the Berchtesgaden path: The Prime Minister on his way to see the Fuehrer about Nazi Germany's menacing designs on Czechoslovakia. On Chamberlain's return from his first visit to Hitler, a deputation consisting of Walter Citrine, Herbert Morrison and Hugh Dalton called on him to re-affirm that both the industrial and political wings of the labour Movement were determined to support the Government in opposition to Hitler's demands.

A "No Appeasement" demonstration in Trafalgar Square. The 1938 Trades Union Congress had passed a declaration, drafted jointly by the Labour Party and the T.U.C., which urged the British Government to stand firm whatever the risks of war might be, and to act with the French and Soviet Governments in proclaiming their determination to stand by Czechoslovakia if she were attacked.

*"I am ready to chance a world war and I would rather have it now. I am forty-nine and I want to be able to lead my people." This, said Chamberlain to the Citrine deputation, was what Hitler had told him at their meeting.*

# Autumn, 1938: Neville Chamberlain forecasts 'Peace in our time'

*July 1939. At the T.U.C. annual summer school, at Ruskin College, Oxford, Sir Walter Citrine answers students' questions. There were plenty of questions to ask. In March, Hitler, to the pained surprise of Chamberlain and Halifax, had seized the whole of Czechoslovakia. In the same month the National Council of Labour had called upon the British Government to make the sort of pact with France and the Soviet Union that alone was likely to halt Hitler in his predatory advance across Europe. Shortly afterwards, the General Council had been consulted by the Government about plans for mobilisation, and about a Schedule of Reserved Occupations. But by May, when a conference of trade union executives met to endorse the measures envisaged, the Government had determined to introduce conscription: a decision against which the conference felt impelled to protest.*

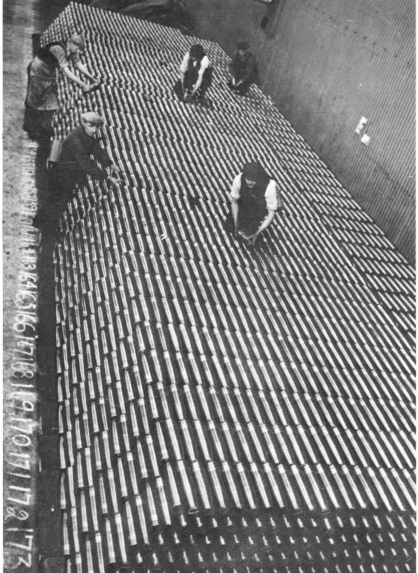

*After years of debate Britain's munitions factories at last start to work flat out. The T.U.C. whose representatives were just gathering for the 1939 Congress at Bridlington when the blitzkrieg against Poland was launched, issued an unequivocal declaration of support for the war against Hitler, proclaiming—"The defeat of ruthless aggression is essential if liberty and order are to be re-established in the world. Congress, with a united and resolute nation, enters the struggle with a clear conscience and steadfast purpose."*

At sea, it was British convoys that first felt the full impact of the Nazis' U-boats.

Representatives of the T.U.C. and the employers under the chairmanship of the Minister of Labour get together in October, 1939, to advise the Government on the administration of war-time industry. The National Joint Advisory Council to the Minister of Labour, as the Committee was called, still provides a means for the Government to regularly consult both sides of industry on industrial issues.

# Total war begins—and Churchill enlists full TUC and Labour Party participation in Government and war effort

*Spring, 1940. In May, the "phoney war" explodes into reality with Hitler's invasion of the Low Countries, and the blast of the explosion sweeps Chamberlain from the Premiership. Winston Churchill, as Prime Minister, invites Ernest Bevin, who is not as yet a Member of Parliament, to take over the Ministry of Labour. He also invites Clement Attlee and Arthur Greenwood to become members of the War Cabinet.*
*Forthwith, the General Council of the T.U.C. and the Executive of the Transport and General Workers' Union approve Bevin's proposed acceptance of the invitation. On May 13th,*

*Bevin writes, characteristically, to Churchill:—"I want, however, in accepting Office to emphasise what I said on Saturday that I feel it is imperative that (the Ministry of Labour's) position and place should be strengthened in order to deal with the problem of labour organisation and supply, and that the Ministry must be in a position to make its contribution to the actual organisation of production so as to secure the right utilisation of Labour and not merely to be regarded as an institution to supply the personnel".*
*Shortly afterwards, the Ministry of Labour is expanded into Ministry of Labour and National Service.*

# Wartime consultation sets the pattern for peacetime planning

DURING the last lap of the T.U.C.'s first hundred years run, full employment, long a high priority of the trade union Movement, became accepted as a policy objective by all political parties and Governments. This development accounts for many of the T.U.C.'s actions, particularly in the field of economic policy in these years. It created an underlying need for co-operation between Governments and the trade union Movement, particularly if full employment, with its tendency to generate inflationary pressures, was to be reconciled with the other main objective of trade unions to secure real improvements in the living standards of working people, especially in Britain's strained post-war economic circumstances.

The processes of consultation between the T.U.C. and the appropriate unions and all relevant Ministries were re-established, more completely than ever before, during the years of the second world war. And the T.U.C. became involved in almost every aspect of the war effort, particularly in mobilising the nation's resources through joint committees set up with every major Government Department.

To meet the demands of war, trade union organisation in the regions was strengthened through the creation of T.U.C. Regional Advisory Committees consisting of full-time union officers drawn from the unions in the area. And the T.U.C. leaned more and more on its local agents—the Trades Councils—when the Government asked for representatives to serve on local committees dealing with such issues as price control and food rationing.

At the same time the General Council busied itself with major studies of the policies that would be needed for post-war reconstruction. A solid foundation for such policies had been laid in the decade before the war; but the T.U.C. now began to examine the implications of full employment, and to consider the case for wage restraint as a means of sustaining real incomes in the context of a threat of inflation.

In the event, the post-war Labour Government drew freely on the T.U.C.'s research and draft plans for the public ownership of the nation's basic industries and the 1945-1950 Attlee Government's implementation of policies closely aligned with those of the T.U.C. on social welfare were landmarks in the development of the Welfare State. For its part, the trade union Movement at large now became even more closely associated with the administration of the social services.

The loyalty of most trade unions to a Labour Government assisted the T.U.C. in supporting the Government policies on wage restraint, as presented to a Conference of Trade Union Executives by Sir Stafford Cripps in March, 1948. The support was given subject to the clear proviso that trade union co-operation must be conditional upon the Government's vigorous and firm pursuit of "a policy designed not only to stabilise but to reduce profits and prices".

In 1949 Congress adopted a General Council Report stating that they "would be failing in their duty if they did not make it unmistakably clear that there is no possibility of securing any widespread and sweeping price reductions." Nevertheless, after the 1949 devaluation of the pound the General Council continued to support the Government's policies for dealing with the crisis in the balance of payments and for maintaining full employment. They stated at this time that it was necessary "to urge unions to exercise even greater restraint on wage demands in the future than they had exercised in the past".

But with the onset of the Korean war prices soared. And this moved the T.U.C.'s constituent unions to carry at the 1950 Congress a resolution calling upon the General Council to abandon the policy of wage restraint.

The return of a Conservative Government to power, with a slim majority, in 1951, found the T.U.C. continuing to maintain a working relationship with the Government of the day.

The new Government faced commitments of a very different nature from those which had existed when the Conservatives had last been in office before 1940. From being on the fringe of industry doing little but hold the ring while the combatants get on with the struggle inside it, the Government was now firmly expected to manage the economy. From administering a piecemeal and somewhat arbitrary system of social benefits, the Government was now responsible for an all embracing and solidly established Welfare State. From having a few pockets of industry under its direct control like the Post Office and Royal Ordnance factories the Government was now responsible for a number of major industries including the giants of fuel, power and transport.

Slowly the Conservative Government adjusted to the new situation but not without abandoning many of their previous policies. What could be altered to meet Conservative beliefs without too much damage to public administration was altered, however, what could not be altered without seriously harming the national economy was not.

So much so that by the 1964 election, 13 years later, the Conservative Government had introduced special measures to influence the economic development of the regions, established the National Economic Development Council with the intention of working towards some planning of the economy, kept a new industry like nuclear energy firmly in public ownership, and passed an Act to levy employers to pay for industrial training. On the debit side, however, they had dismantled much of the planning network which had been set up during and immediately after the war, and cut the services of the Ministry of Labour at a time when they should have been expanding to facilitate the movement of labour between trades and industries.

But inevitably on balance over these years a much closer relationship developed between the T.U.C. and Government. Recurring balance of payments crises and the failure of the economy to grow at the rate achieved elsewhere in the world compelled the

Government to intervene more readily and directly in the economy, thus creating a need for closer consultation with the representative bodies of both sides of industry, in order to elicit their support for Government measures and make use of their experience and expertise in deciding what measures to take and how best to implement them.

Successive attempts to start a new dialogue with the T.U.C. on economic problems were generally accompanied by unilateral Governmental pressures on wages which successfully prevented the conversation from properly starting.

With the return of a Labour Government in 1964, however, things which had been pending became pointed. The new Government made it clear that it hoped for, and expected, maximum action and co-operation from industry—and especially from the trade unions.

The very fact that the Labour Government attempted to manage the economy with the aim of providing long term economic growth combined with full employment and a satisfactory balance of payments involved a considerable extension of those frontiers between Government and unions along which issues of concern to both parties were liable to arise. On such issues the interests of Government and trade unions did not automatically coincide. Consequently, disagreements developed as to how best to deal with particular questions.

The major difference was over whether individuals in a free society should be coerced to work in situations or on terms which they found unacceptable.

The T.U.C. all along contended that ultimately most differences between Government and voluntary organisations had to be settled by discussion and compromise. A government's job was to govern; but its authority to compel organisations and individuals to follow a certain course of action was limited in practice by the extent to which compulsion was accepted in a democracy as necessary by the individuals and organisations concerned. And the T.U.C. pointed out that "the national

interest" as defined by others was often either "the Government's interest", or some sectional interest, disguised in a patriotic mask.

Thus, in its recent evidence to the Royal Commission on Trade Unions and Employers' Associations the General Council of the T.U.C. observed:— "The interests of different individuals and groups diverge in many respects. Where this is so, some groups clearly think it is effective propaganda to claim that their policy corresponds to, or reflects, the national interest, and that other groups ought likewise to take account of the national interest. However successful in the propaganda battle such advocacy might be, it is almost invariably based on myths, and a few moments' consideration would convince the disinterested observer, if such could be found, that this was so.

"Trade unionists, therefore, take a somewhat jaundiced view of those whose interests are different from their own lecturing them on their social responsibilities, with the real intention of providing a result which is favourable to themselves."

The need to arrive at acceptable compromises on the large number of issues of concern to both government and industry if the objective of stable economic growth was to be attained led to major developments in the T.U.C.'s relationships with employers and with its own affiliated trade unions.

The influence of the National Economic Development Council on the whole range of the Government's economic and industrial policies depended to some extent on the measure of understanding that could be reached between the employers and the T.U.C. The regular meetings between the T.U.C. and Confederation of British Industry (recalling some forty years later the attempts, albeit then ill-fated, of the Mond-Turner initiative) have already led to an examination of many economic questions of interest to both bodies.

With the establishment of the National Economic Development Council and of Economic Development Committees in

specific industries the T.U.C. became involved in the details of economic development. By this time the T.U.C. was well equipped for framing general policies but inevitably when it came to influencing collective agreements, or discussing research and investment policies in a particular industry, it was bound to bear more and more heavily upon co-operation and assistance of the unions.

An important step in the co-operation between the T.U.C. and its unions has been in the development of incomes policy, following the signing of the "Statement of Intent" in December 1964. At the 1965 Congress the General Council were given authority to review union wage claims in the light of Congress policy. That development in itself immediately brought the T.U.C. into discussions with individual unions about specific issues relating to productivity, manpower, wage-payment systems, the system of collective bargaining, and many other matters.

So, as the T.U.C.'s first century of activity drew to a close, some significant, and perhaps momentous, developments were taking place in the relationships between the T.U.C. and its affiliated unions.

For one thing, the General Council had been given some authority to seek to influence the policies of individual unions so that they would take into account the over-riding objectives of the wider trade union Movement.

For another, the T.U.C.'s increasing economic responsibilities inevitably led it to be in much closer touch with the individual unions on other issues such as trade union methods, trade union organisation and the provision of union services. It is in this area that one of the T.U.C.'s major tasks lies as it moves into its second century. ∎

Shipbuilding and other industries vital to the war effort become classified as "Essential Work". Until Ernest Bevin took over the Ministry of Labour, employers had been bidding against each other for available labour, and no scale of national priorities for the use of manpower existed.

Bevin's Restriction of Engagement Order put a stop to this haphazard form of poaching by employers. Nevertheless, by the autumn of 1940, the shortage of skilled labour had become acute. So, in the spring of 1941 the Essential Work (General Provisions) Order was made, providing for a register of skilled workers and for their direction, where necessary, into "essential" employment.

Workers in undertakings engaged on essential work were covered by rules laying down minimum requirements for wages, conditions and welfare; and though they could not leave their jobs without Ministry of Labour permission, they could not be dismissed from them, either.

Below: Families in a blitzed area queue for water from a fire hydrant. With supplies of water, food and fuel often disrupted, local committees which included nominees from Trades Councils helped to prevent the outrageous inequalities of the first world war in the distribution of essential supplies.

# Coalition—and the Government calls in the unions

DURING the war years T.U.C. co-operation with the Government really got off the ground both at national level and in the detailed administration of policy throughout the country. The Government did not immediately realise that the T.U.C. was essential to the war effort, but it did not take them long to come to that point of view. What they probably never realised was the profound effects that this would have on relations between the unions and the Government in the post-war years.

At first the Government were hesitant in seeking to consult trade unions on mobilising Britain's industry for war. A major failure of the Chamberlain Government was when the Ministry of Supply was established in July 1939 and an Advisory Industrial Panel was appointed consisting exclusively of industrialists and business men, with no representation from trade unions. After the T.U.C. took the issue to the Prime Minister he issued a circular to all Government Departments stating that the Government wished the representatives of trade unions to be consulted on all matters of concern to them. A Central Advisory Committee composed equally of employers and trade union representatives was immediately established to work with the Ministry of Supply and the three Service Departments. On taking office, Churchill reiterated this instruction to all Government Departments.

These early war measures were rapidly followed by the formation of a number of national bodies composed of representatives from Government, the employers and the trade unions. The National Joint Advisory Council to the Minister of Labour was established in 1939 as a purely advisory body, but more significant, day-to-day consultation was carried out by the N.J.A.C.'s offshoot, the Joint Consultative Committee set up by Ernest Bevin eight days after becoming Minister of Labour. This body enabled trade unions to exert a considerable influence on future war measures, notably those concerning the Government's policy on direction of labour and conditions in the nation's workshops.

Numerous other advisory bodies were formed during 1939 and 1940. On the T.U.C. Advisory Committee to the Ministry of Food, and the Central Price Regulation Committee of the Board of Trade, for example, trade union representatives discussed regulations governing the rationing of food and clothes which were gradually extended following union pressure. By 1943 the T.U.C. was giving detailed advice on complex rationing arrangements, including the provision of special rationing allowances, particularly for groups of workers doing heavy manual work.

Further, in 1941 close co-operation between the trade union Movement and the Supply and Service Departments of the Government was ensured through the new Central Joint Advisory Committee to the Production Executive of the Cabinet. In addition to all this, the Government established simultaneously regional machinery of administration to deal with the efficient execution of war policies. Area Boards, which in 1941 became Regional Production Boards, co-ordinated the efforts of all the Government officials in each area on matters such as the production of essential goods and the supply of munitions.

But the Government's regional organisation was designed not only to carry into effect the policies on price control and rationing: it was also intended to operate under a government official, known as a Regional Commissioner, as an alternative form of government in the event of the breakdown of national government following invasion.

For its part the T.U.C. decided in 1941 to duplicate the Government machinery in the regions. The country had been divided into 12 Defence Regions and in each of these the T.U.C. appointed 12 trade union representatives to advise the Commissioner on industry and production and formed Emergency Committees of union full-time officers. They functioned as an important channel of communication between the General Council and full-time officers throughout the country and were continued in the post-war years when the committees were re-convened in 1945 as peacetime Regional Advisory Committees to "act as the agent of the T.U.C. and undertake such industrial duties and investigations as may be required by the General Council from time to time".

By the end of the war, for a second time, a generation of trade union officers at national and local level had learnt in numerous governmental committees and public authorities to use their industrial experience to further the efficient use and equitable distribution of the nation's scarce resources. But this time they were not to be demobilised. With the peace, the Labour Government expected trade unions to continue to give advice and assist in administering essential public services. In particular they were to be closely associated with the running of the new and expanded social services.

# Hitler invades Russia and the TUC organises Soviet aid . . .

THE GERMAN armies invaded the Soviet Union in June, 1941, and the British Government decided to give the Russians the only kind of aid which was practicable at the time. A "Second Front" being ruled out on strategic grounds they sent a flow of tanks and guns and other war supplies, which they could ill afford, in a series of hazardous convoys to Murmansk. These supplies were themselves made possible by the colossal productive efforts of British working people; and by the successful operations of the Central Advisory Production Committee (which had been set up with trade union representation); of the regional production boards; and of the Joint Workshop Production Committees at factory level.

With the invasion of Russia the General Council immediately proposed an Anglo-Russian Trade Union Council to exchange views and information on the problems facing the trade union Movement in each country. The National Council of Labour followed up by launching a "Help for Russia" fund. The fund, administered by the T.U.C., raised over £800,000 during the remaining war years—and 19s. 11¾d. in every £1 was spent on actual purchases for the Russian people.

*Members of the armed forces despatch medical supplies to M. Shvernik, Moscow. The supplies were purchased with money contributed to the "Help for Russia" fund launched by the National Council of Labour in 1941.*

*1942. Walter Citrine (right) takes a party of Soviet delegates of the Anglo-Russian Trade Union Committee round British war factories. To the right of Citrine: M. Shvernik, Secretary of the All-Union Central Council of Trade Unions, shakes hands with a British worker.*

*Victory in Europe and the lights go up again in London; victory in Japan and a cloud overshadows the peace.*

# ...and plans post-war reconstruction

WITH the "end of the beginning" of the war the 1943 Trades Union Congress in Southport passed a resolution which registered deep concern lest the end of the war found the nation no better prepared for the tasks of peace than it had been for those of war. Already there was growing public support for major educational reforms that owed much to the advocacy of the Campaign for Educational Advance, an organisation formed in November, 1952, by the T.U.C., the Co-operative Union, the National Union of Teachers and the Workers' Educational Association. In other fields, too, the T.U.C. was beginning to make an independent examination of the problems of post-war reconstruction and was represented on many governmental committees engaged in similar studies, and by the next Congress at Blackpool the "Interim Report on Post-war Reconstruction" was ready. Among other things, it sought to explain how the British working people who, whether in or out of uniform, were then fully employed in the war could be equally fully employed in peace.

"Full employment as defined by Sir William Beveridge," the report said, "namely a situation in which 'though on any one day there may be some men unemployed, there are always more vacant jobs than there are unemployed men, so that every man whose present job comes to an end for any reason can find fresh employment without delay,' is a general objective to which the trade union Movement subscribes. This does not imply, however, that the trade unions would approve *any* policy which might be likely to achieve this objective ...

"Whilst we recognise that a disciplined observance of collective agreements and a high degree of mobility of labour between occupations are necessary to the permanent maintenance of a condition of full employment, we do not consider that compulsory arbitration or direction of labour are required or are in any way desirable. *Providing the Government was able to give adequate guarantees that it was genuinely pursuing a policy of full employment and was determined to take all necessary steps to control prices and otherwise prevent the exploitation of the situation by private interests, the trade unions would undertake to avoid wage policies and demarcation or other practices which might impede the achievement of full employment ...*"

To get Government and trade unionists to pursue the policies set out in this Report has been the paramount interest of the T.U.C. not only in the immediate post-war years but in the subsequent two decades.

Clement Attlee addresses the 1945 Congress in Blackpool shortly after the General Election, when 393 Labour M.P.s, including 120 trade union sponsored candidates, were returned to the Commons and Attlee became Prime Minister. On his right are Walter Citrine and Ebby Edwards who were to be appointed by the Government to serve on the board of the newly nationalised coal industry.

# The Welfare State is born and the TUC

"WITH the exception of one point there is little difference between my proposals and the proposals of the T.U.C." So said Sir William Beveridge in 1942 on the publication of his Report—the blueprint for virtually the entire programme of social legislation enacted in the next few years. The point of difference, however, was relatively small.

The T.U.C. advocated a compensation for industrial accidents scheme entirely separate from National Insurance. Beveridge wanted the two merged and his argument won the day.

The T.U.C. did not find so much agreement, however, when it came to implementing the Beveridge proposals. For two years an energetic campaign was waged for action by the Coalition Government. But the T.U.C. had to await the 1945 landslide Labour victory before Beveridge's comprehensive social security system, embodying a unified National Insurance scheme for sickness and unemployment, family allowances, a National Health Service, industrial injuries compensation and a National Assistance service, began to take shape.

The T.U.C. had every right to the title —again bestowed by Sir William—of "the Godfathers of the Beveridge Report". Back in the early days of the war the Secretary of the T.U.C. Social Insurance Committee worked closely with Beveridge on social security plans and the General Council were instrumental in getting the official Interdepartmental Committee set up which subsequently published the Report.

In itself this is not surprising. Trade unions had for decades been administering social benefits for their members and along with insurance companies were the most qualified to advise the Government on the myriad of matters which launching a new social security system entailed. And they did so. Deputation after deputation went to Whitehall, first with demands for a statement of the Government's intentions and then later with detailed suggestions on how the scheme should work. As well as this, Aneurin Bevan, as Minister of Health, was later to comment on the immense help given by the T.U.C. Social Insurance Department with the National Health Service Bill and to request more "specific assistance" from the T.U.C. Yet if the T.U.C. had a dispute with any Minister over social welfare it was with the Minister of Health. Disappointment at the failure to include an industrial health service in the National Health Service was frequently expressed to the Minister. But he was not to be moved and the T.U.C.'s proposals for a comprehensive occupational health service seeking out the causes of sickness in industry, advising on prevention and

*Sir William Beveridge, author of the report on which the welfare state was based.*

*J. L. Smyth, T.U.C. Social Insurance Secretary, who at the invitation of the Minister of National Insurance, the Rt. Hon. James Griffiths, left the T.U.C. in 1946 to become Industrial Adviser with the Ministry.*

*Aneurin Bevan, first Minister of Health.*

# amed as Godfather

providing a medical service at work are still to be acted upon.

Since 1946 successive Governments have continued to consult the T.U.C. about major changes in social security legislation, and trade union nominees have been actively associated with the day-to-day working of the social security schemes and the hospital service through membership of appropriate local committees and tribunals. Local trades councils were given a major responsibility for nominating representatives of workers to serve on many of these bodies. The significance of the work of the local tribunals, for example, is reflected in the 40,000 disputed claims heard every year before the 200 National Insurance Local Appeal Tribunals. A total of 3,000 trade union nominees now serve on Appeal Tribunals and on top of this many of the appellants are represented by trade union officials.

*Included in the Government's social security provisions was the Industrial Injuries Act which insured all workers against accidents arising at work in a national system based on contributions from employers and employees. In the picture below, trapped in the twisted metal of the collapsed scaffolding, two men lie dead and two others are seriously injured.*

# The cold war chills union attempts at international co-operation

*Fresh start in Hamburg. Following the post-war resuscitation of the German building workers' free trade union, Richard Burmester cleanses the city's trade union building of its Swastika.*

*Some of the leaders of the newly formed World Federation of Trade Unions, at a special reception which General de Gaulle held for them in Paris in the late autumn of 1945. From left, Hillman of the United States, Citrine of Great Britain and Jouhaux of France.*

WHILST the West and East were doing their best to make the most of the immediate post-war honeymoon, the world's trade unions joined together to form the World Federation of Trade Unions. The initiative was taken by the T.U.C. General Council who convened a World Trade Union Conference in London in February 1945 to discuss the creation of a new international trade union organisation.

The W.F.T.U. had been designed, hopefully, as a world-wide body embracing non-communist unions which had hitherto belonged to the I.F.T.U., and communist unions, hitherto members of the Red International of Labour

*The construction in 1948 of the great Abbey Works Steel Mill in South Wales, to which American aid contributed 27 million dollars worth of equipment. The Marshall Plan for the provision of American aid to Europe was violently opposed by the communists in the World Federation of Trade Unions.*

Unions. The hopes were shortlived. In 1949, finding that the W.F.T.U. was being used as a rostrum for communist propaganda, the British, American and Dutch unions withdrew, and later founded the International Confederation of Free Trade Unions.

In 1945, even before the last Nazis fell, the T.U.C. was also helping to re-establish effective trade union organisation in war-devastated Europe. The German trade union Movement had been suppressed by Hitler and most trade union leaders were annihilated.

The General Council were quick to respond to a call for advice in establishing a new German Movement. The Germans, freed from the hindrance of history and the problems of compromising between long-established unions, were able to build a model trade union Movement reflecting the idea of one union for each major industry.

In Greece the problems of establishing an effective trade union Movement proved more intractable. The outbreak of Civil War in December 1944 led to rival factions claiming to represent Greek workers, and this situation was made more difficult by the repressive measures of the Greek Government. In February 1945 a T.U.C. delegation arrived in Greece at the invitation of some Greek trade unions, and it was the end of June before the last member of the T.U.C. team left after finally getting agreement among the different groups about the holding of elections among Greek workers to choose bona fide union representatives. But continual repression by the Greek Government and conflicts between different groups of trade unionists meant that the difficulties facing the trade union Movement in Greece were not overcome until the end of the Civil War four years later.

*Grantly Adams of Barbados, and Vincent Tewson, General Secretary of the T.U.C., at the inaugural conference in London of the International Confederation of Free Trade Unions, November, 1949, following the withdrawal by a number of trade union Movements from the W.F.T.U., which had become dominated by communists bent upon waging the cold war. The Conference resolved to give its full backing to the implementation of the European Recovery Programme (the Marshall Plan) and to do all it could to nurture the growth of trade union Movements in underdeveloped countries.*

The particularly savage weather and persistent blizzards of early 1947 prevented many coal trains from moving and effectively brought much of industry to a stop. When the next winter came power still had to be cut because of short supply despite efforts by volunteer railwaymen to speed the turn-round of coal-carrying railway wagons.

# Public industries have a bleak beginning in the 1947 freeze-up

During the fuel crisis. A young citizen of Poplar waits outside the gasworks, while his elder brother goes inside, in the hope of getting some coke.

Down at the coal face in the 1940's. In the next quarter of a century the National Coal Board was to bring about a revolution in getting coal, which eventually culminated in a single machine controlled at the press of a button which cuts, loads and conveys the coal from the face, whilst constructing its own tunnel.

THE BEGINNING of 1947 saw the National Coal Board assuming responsibility for managing the mines for the nation. During the year Parliament was also to pass the Act nationalising the transport industry. But in 1947 these industries were soon in trouble. The unusually severe winter brought a paralysing fuel crisis which brought much of the country's industrial activity to a standstill. Winter thus dramatically exposed Britain's economic problem of balancing its international trading payments to a degree sufficient to satisfy foreign holders of sterling. The foreign exchange crisis which followed in the summer led to restrictions on the convertibility of sterling into dollars.

The T.U.C. responded to the crisis by agreeing to the Government's policy on wage restraint and to the re-introduction of a Control of Engagements Order which placed legal restraints on workers changing their jobs. But the T.U.C. also called for an extension of workers participation in industry with the revival of the factory joint production committees which had proved so fruitful during the war.

The question of trade union and workers participation in the management of the nation's industries had been an issue on which the T.U.C. had differed from the Labour Government's nationalisation proposals. On fuel and power Emanuel Shinwell, as Minister, asked the T.U.C. in October 1945 to set up a small committee to advise him, and there was close co-operation with the Minister on his large nationalisation programme.

Despite the talks the General Council did not get things all their own way. The Act nationalising the coal industry did not provide for the statutory appointment of representatives of workers in the National Coal Board as they had advocated. However, the Minister was to go further than he was required by the Act and two trade union leaders were appointed to the Board—Sir Walter Citrine and Ebby Edwards who was secretary of the mineworkers. Citrine became a peer and was succeeded as General Secretary of the T.U.C. by Vincent Tewson. Later Lord Citrine was to become Chairman of the Central Electricity Authority.

The General Council were also at odds with the Minister over the Bill for nationalising the mines because it said nothing about setting up consultative machinery on matters other than wages and hours. The T.U.C. Post-war Reconstruction Report's suggestion was for consultative councils that could discuss all matters of policy for the industry and would include workers' representatives chosen through existing union organisations. And subsequently, after T.U.C. pressure, a clause was added to the Bill whilst it was going through Parliament. It provided for the establishment of joint machinery through which questions could be raised on safety or welfare and all matters concerning the industry of mutual interest to the N.C.B. and its employees. Similar provision was made in the other nationalisation Acts.

It was not until nearly twenty years had passed that the T.U.C. again found itself face to face with the Government on the issue of workers' participation, when nationalisation proposals for the iron and steel industry were put forward a second time.

Meanwhile, the T.U.C.'s attitude to industrial democracy had altered. In its evidence to the Royal Commission on Trade Unions and Employers' Associations, it extended its belief in workers' participation both within public industry and—more significantly —in private industry. Behind this was the more explicit assumption that the function of trade unions was identical whoever owned the industry. The Commission was urged to recommend that any legal obstacles to trade union representation on the boards of private companies should be removed. And the evidence advocated a great extension of workers' participation in public industry, so that union representatives were directly involved in the management of these industries at every level and not merely consulted about the decisions which management intended to take.

With the setting up of the British Steel Corporation in 1967 came an experiment in workers' participation in the public sector by providing for workers' directors on the industry's four group boards.

For its part, the T.U.C. was anxious to encourage experiments with different forms of trade union participation in industry. At the same time public concern that trade unions should accept greater responsibility for industrial efficiency was creating a new awareness of the need for improvements in joint consultation in industry and a widening of the scope of negotiations.

*October, 1947. Two men with their minds on the expansion of exports and the drastic restriction of home consumption: Sir Stafford Cripps, the new Minister for Economic Affairs, and Mr. Harold Wilson, who had just taken his place as President of the Board of Trade.*

"I'LL ATTEND TO THE FOUNDATIONS LATER"

"HMM... HORSE 20$\frac{4}{15}$, JOCKEY 20$\frac{5}{15}$.  GOING TO BE A CLOSE THING."

TIMING THE FAVOURITE

**THE OLD HORSE DOESN'T LIKE BEING FENCED IN**

How David Low saw the TUC—
as an endearing horse, 'given to
remarkable feats of activity,
climbing high mountains of recovery,
jumping high fences of production
and pulling huge loads of export'

*By kind permission of the Evening Standard.*

# Productivity: the key word in post-war Britain

*Members of the Anglo-American Council on Productivity Team from British Industry, including union officials, seen here during a visit to the Blaw-Knox and Co. steel works, Pittsburgh, U.S.A. in 1950.*

*The end of the open hearth. Project Spear, the reconstruction of the Rotherham plant of the Steel, Peech & Tozer Co., included automatic loading of electric furnaces as part of a production line technique controlled through a central panel showing all the different stages of production. The company was taken into public ownership in 1967 and its Rotherham works are now part of the Midland Group of the British Steel Corporation.*

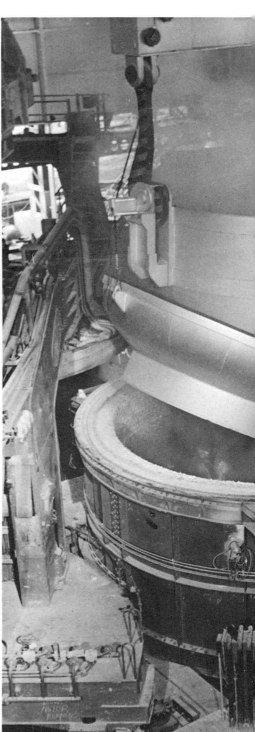

"UNTIL Joint Production Committees —later re-named Joint Consultative Committees—were introduced during the second world war, British trade unions had a tradition against associating themselves with joint bodies formed to stimulate higher output . . ." wrote G. D. H. Cole. "In trade union nostrils, the word 'productivity' smelt of 'speeding-up' and breaking down cherished craft customs: it suggested scientific management, efficiency experts and industrial consultant firms such as Bedaux . . ."

With the end of the second world war, though, 'productivity' started to be presented in some quarters as an almost magical panacea for all the post-war world's economic ailments. To the T.U.C. 'productivity' was not such a simple matter as that. For them it involved an examination in depth of many questions such as investment, scientific research, supply of manpower, regional development, economic policy, wage payment systems and payment-by-results, the use of management techniques, and productivity bargaining. The development of production policies by the T.U.C. was furthered by the setting up of the T.U.C. Production Committee and Department in 1950, at a time when far-reaching changes in technology and management practice were beginning to take place. And in the ensuing years increasing emphasis has been placed by governments on the need for modernisation and efficiency in every workplace. Adaptation and change have become key factors. The department's contribution to the training of union officers and representatives in production and management subjects was to bring about a better understanding by unions of the significance of these issues and help them to handle them in negotiations. The work of the Production Committee has contributed to bringing employers, as well as governments and specialised agencies concerned with management and production matters, to appreciate the need to take workers' interests into account when considering measures to increase productivity.

Another word that became increasingly used to gloss over the problem of industrial development was "automation." In 1956 in a major statement on the subject the T.U.C. pointed out that automation was neither new in itself nor in the problems it produced, for problems had always arisen every time a new machine had displaced human labour—which had been going on throughout the industrial revolutions of the 19th and 20th centuries. The report dwelt particularly upon some of the social issues arising from rapid technological change such as redundancy, the need for re-deployment and re-training of labour and the difficulties arising from any increase in shift work. Yet at the same time as the T.U.C. was pressing these points, the Government was allowing the Ministry of Labour services, including re-training centres, to deteriorate.

The report also drew attention to the problems of spreading the benefits of automation throughout the community and to the social gains that would accrue from using increased productivity to reduce prices to consumers.

"In the absence of suitable joint industrial or Government machinery for discussing or negotiating on consumer prices," it said, "it may be that, as consumers, trade unionists will have to be prepared to see the prices of some commodities and services rise (i.e. commodities and services produced in industries where there is little scope for automation) to accommodate their demands as producers and union members for uniform improvements in working and social conditions." The fact was that whilst Governments constantly looked for ways to restrain the growth of wages nothing effective had been done to limit the constant rise in prices. This situation compelled trade unions to concentrate their attentions on wage bargaining and distracted them from giving more detailed consideration to productivity.

*In July, 1950, a shooting war broke out in Korea and in Britain the cost of living, which had been rising gradually in the wake of the Labour Government's 1949 devaluation of the pound, started to soar as a consequence of the war leading inevitably to the end of the T.U.C.'s wage restraint policies.*

# Korea helps Tories to power in "this age of clatter and buzz, of gape and gloat"

THE T.U.C.'s declared expectations about continued consultation with the Government were by and large respected by the new Minister of Labour, Sir Walter Monckton, and by the Chancellor of the Exchequer, Mr. R. A. Butler, who took care to consult the T.U.C.'s Economic Committee on practically all subjects that could be of concern to them although there were major differences on policy. Only once, when Monckton's reference-back of the various pay awards proposed by Wages Councils threatened a major dislocation of the established wage determining machinery, did the T.U.C. feel it necessary to intervene, directly and successfully, with the Prime Minister.

The T.U.C. also successfully appealed to the Prime Minister over the head of Dame Florence Horsbrugh, the Minister of Education, about her intention to make a 10 per cent. cut in the Ministry's grants for adult education services. In his reply to the T.U.C. Winston Churchill wrote:

"There is perhaps no branch of our vast educational system which should more attract within its particular sphere the aid and encouragement of the State than adult education. How many there must be in Britain, after the disturbance of two destructive wars, who thirst in later life to learn about the humanities, the history of their country, the philosophies of the human race, and the arts and letters which sustain and are borne forward by the ever-conquering English language? . . . I have no doubt myself that a man or woman earnestly seeking in grown-up life to be guided to wide and suggestive knowledge in its largest and most uplifted sphere will make the best of all the pupils in this age of clatter and buzz, of gape and gloat. The appetite of adults to be shown the foundations and processes of thought will never be denied by a British Administration cherishing the continuity of our island life."

*The last months of the Labour Government were marked by the opening on London's South Bank of the Festival of Britain, 100 years after the Great Exhibition of Victorian times. The Royal Festival Hall, scene of the T.U.C. Centenary Concert on June 7, 1968, is to the right of the tower.*

*After the General Election of 1951, Winston Churchill became Premier, with a narrow Conservative majority in the House of Commons and he appointed Sir Walter Monckton to the post of Minister of Labour. The General Council of the T.U.C. proceeded publicly to define its position in relation to the new Government. "Since the Conservative administration of pre-war days" the General Council declared, "the range of consultation between Ministers and both sides of industry has considerably increased, and the machinery of joint consultation has enormously improved. We expect of this Government that they will maintain to the full this practice of consultation. On our part, we shall continue to examine every question solely in the light of its industrial and economic implications".*

*Budapest on the morrow of the Russian invasion against the Hungarian freedom fighters.*

# The TUC sends aid to Hungary and condemns the Suez adventure

WITH a great deal of British and French military help Israel was on the Suez Canal in ten days after crushing the Egyptian army in the Sinai desert. Russian tanks took about as long to crush the rising in Hungary.

Appalled by both these events, the T.U.C. joined with the other sections of the Labour Movement in condemning the British Government for resorting to armed force against Egypt and launched its own appeal backed by a million leaflets to raise aid for the victims of the Soviet repression in Hungary.

By the end of the first month in November 1956 £50,000 had been raised which was converted into medical aid and rushed to Hungary through the International Confederation of Free Trade Unions.

Despite the response, spare money was becoming harder to find. The retail price index rose again after the Suez adventure as the shortage of oil and the closure of the canal added to costs. But in a few months the report of Lord Cohen on Prices, Productivity and Incomes supported the view of Harold Macmillan's Government that wage increases at the time would be highly undesirable.

The events in Hungary had another effect, however, on the British trade union Movement. A number of prominent trade union leaders resigned from the Communist Party in protest against the Soviet action. Their resignations followed more than a decade of rancorous debate about the purpose of trade unionism and communist influence within the trade union Movement which moved some unions to exclude Communist Party members from office.

The rancour was not to finish there, though. Three years later charges of ballot rigging were levelled at the communist leadership of the Electrical Trades Union and the T.U.C., after three years of patient attempts to get the E.T.U. to deal with the allegations, expelled the E.T.U. from membership at the 1961 Congress.

Not that this was in itself a political issue. As the T.U.C. general secretary said at the time: "The people who did this may have been communists, but I am not criticizing them, nor are the General Council, because they are communists. We are criticizing them because they were implicated in fraud." The perpetrators of the fraud were subsequently removed from office following judgment in the High Court, and the E.T.U. membership elected new national officials. The union reaffiliated to the T.U.C. in the following year.

Lancaster House, London, and Prime Minister Sir Anthony Eden on the eve of the Suez crisis, and shortly before his resignation.

Port Said at the entrance to the Suez Canal where British invasion troops landed during the 'armed conflict' with Egypt.

*Congress House in Bloomsbury: headquarters of the T.U.C. An immediate impression of elegant simplicity, of spaciousness and light. The design of the building was the subject of an open architectural competition, won by the architect David du R Aberdeen, in 1948. A bronze medal was awarded to Congress House in 1959 by the Royal Institute of the British Architects.*

# The official opening of Congress House, a memori.

"AS A WORK of art, Epstein's group appears to be almost painfully moving. It is a tragic monument on the grand scale.

"The fact that so much thought and money has been devoted to its setting is also of the greatest importance. At a time when old forms of patronage are passing this sets a challenging example." So wrote the "Daily Telegraph" of Epstein's sculpture and the T.U.C.'s action in commissioning it. Yet in the post-war period the T.U.C. was more interested in promoting the arts than in directly sponsoring them.

The war had not long been over before the General Council had made it clear that trade unionism was not just about wages and working conditions.

". . . Beyond day-to-day questions" the 1946 General Council's Report said, "it [the trade union Movement] is concerned with seeing that the worker has the widest opportunities for a full life, and if there are respects in which facilities available to him for the use and enjoyment of his leisure can be improved, in pursuing such improvement."

In a further report in 1961 the General Council reiterated this policy and called for both a widening of educational opportunities so that large numbers of workers would be equipped to participate more fully in cultural activities, and an expansion of public cultural facilities so that more people could enjoy the fine arts, music, film and drama.

A main aim of the T.U.C.'s policy for education had long been secondary education for all children, and to this end the T.U.C. continued to argue the case for raising the school-leaving age to sixteen, and to advocate the widening of educational opportunities for all young people by establishing comprehensive secondary schools.

By the time the Crowther Committee came to present their Report in 1959 on the education of young people from fifteen to eighteen the economic and social arguments for these reforms were overwhelmingly in favour of the views

*Congress House on the day of the opening, March 27, 1958. State trumpeters of the Royal Horse Guards, enrolled as members of the Musicians Union for the occasion, sound a specially commissioned "Congress" fanfare, as Epstein's statue, a memorial to trade unionists killed in two world wars, is unveiled.*

# or the dead, an act of faith for the living

long held by the T.U.C. The political decisions needed to give effect to these views were not to be delayed much longer. In 1964 the Conservative Government announced that the school-leaving age would be raised in 1970–71 and a few months later the Labour Government decided to proceed with reorganisation of secondary education on comprehensive lines. Early in 1968, however, the T.U.C. failed in its efforts to dissuade the Government of the day from postponing for two more years this long-sought-after reform in the post-devaluation economies, though happily the Government's programme for comprehensive schools was safeguarded.

While there has been considerable general improvement in public education, progress with a number of educational reforms long advocated by the T.U.C. has been disappointingly slow. The majority of young workers are still denied day-release from work for further education (as promised in 1944), and successive Governments have failed to expand nursery education, which in the T.U.C.'s opinion would help particularly to offset the limiting effects of adverse social conditions upon many children from working class homes.

Throughout these years the T.U.C. were constantly urging Governments, though with limited success, to share their faith in education.

*Jacob Epstein: an enduring tribute from a genius.*

# The TUC intervenes in industrial disputes

THE TURNING POINT in the T.U.C.'s relations with individual affiliated unions during industrial disputes came in 1955.

Earlier in the decade the T.U.C.'s attitude to "political" strikes had been clearly stated in the introduction to the 1952 General Council's Report. "There is no doubt that many of the steps taken or proposed by the present Government have created a political climate which intensifies the difficulties of trade unions," it said.

"At the same time, with industry playing such an important part in the economic position of the country and in the determination of the standard of living of our people the General Council and the trade union Movement resolutely turned down suggestions that political opposition to the Government and its policy should be reinforced by industrial action."

But during 1955 it was the difficulties of getting to grips with a strike situation before the men actually downed tools which frustrated the General Council.

A national newspaper strike, for example, was called by maintenance engineers and electricians who were outside the industry's negotiating set-up. Both the General Council—and the Court of Inquiry established once the dispute had started—recommended that the unions should be included in central negotiations with the Newspaper Proprietors' Association and on this basis the dispute was settled, but not until the country had been without national newspapers for four weeks.

The railways strike in the same year gave a hint of things to come. This dispute was notified to the T.U.C. by the Associated Society of Locomotive Engineers and Firemen only a few days before the operative strike date. The General Council succeeded, however, in fixing meetings through the Minister of Labour between A.S.L.E.F. and the British Transport Commission which stopped the strike temporarily. But deadlock was again reached and the General Council took on the role which they were now accustomed to play in major disputes—that of "honest broker" seeking to find the common ground on which the parties would find it possible to negotiate a settlement.

After meeting with A.S.L.E.F. and the N.U.R. fresh proposals were put by the T.U.C. to the Minister of Labour who then got talks going again which resulted in the strike being called off after two weeks.

This form of mediation was to set the pattern for the next decade. Congress too saw the sense of it for in the same year it approved the General Council's proposal that they should be able to intervene in a dispute before negotiations had broken down if there was a

*July, 1964: 20,000 postmen assembled in Hyde Park on the day of their one-day strike—the first ever official strike called by the Union of Post Office Workers in its 44 years history.*

June 1966: the queue of ships in the Thames Estuary waiting for berths in the London docks congested by strike-bound vessels as a consequence of the seamen's dispute.

likelihood of other bodies of work-people being affected.

The General Council's new powers to intervene did not however halt the rising number of days lost through strikes. Tempers were running high in the late 1950's as was shown in the six-week printing strike and in the bitter seven-week London bus strike in 1958 when the General Council issued a circular to its unions appealing for funds to support the Transport and General Workers' Union.

In a statement on the 1958 bus strike the General Council said: "Having mismanaged the economy, the Government has chosen the pay claim of London's busmen as an opportunity to put pressure on a public employer to conform to its policy of holding down wages and to bolster the resistance of private employers in whose negotiations with unions it cannot directly interfere."

The T.U.C. had no doubts that the Government's responsibilities for managing the economy included accountability for the effect of its policies. The trouble was that Ministers, anxious to preserve at least some vestige of their traditional economic approach, only accepted those responsibilities when it suited them.

In 1964, for example, the Chancellor of the Exchequer and the Postmaster General went back on their word to accept without reservation the report of the Armitage Committee on postmen's pay and the postmen called a national one-day strike. The Ministry of Labour's conciliation officers were not available, as had been the case before when a Government department was involved, and once more the Government pushed public employees into strike action.

The seamen's dispute in 1966 was the first major strike following the T.U.C.'s acceptance in 1965 of responsibility for operating an incomes policy. The attitudes of the T.U.C. and the Government towards the strike clearly revealed their divergence of views about the nature of incomes policy. The Government under pressure from abroad wanted the maximum restraint and the most rigid application of the policy possible; the T.U.C. saw the practical problems and, therefore, sought to keep the policy as flexible as possible. The executive committee of the Seamen's Union were told, however, that the T.U.C. could not give unqualified support to the claims of any one union, and the General Council proclaimed their right to a view about what was a practical solution in the light of all the circumstances. Eventually the T.U.C.'s efforts contributed to a provisional settlement being reached which included a major inquiry into the causes of the dispute, the terms and conditions of service of seamen, relations between shipowners and seamen, and the Merchant Shipping Act of 1894.

May, 1958: Frank Cousins general secretary of the Transport & General Workers Union addresses a mass meeting of London busmen during the seven week busmen's strike.

143

# 'Trade union structure is a function of purpose'

*Placing a wall panel, an example of industrialised building. On other construction sites the practice of recruiting self-employed workers grew extensively in the late 50's and early 60's. Called "labour-only subcontracting" the system was for an employer to make a contract with a group of workers without materials or plant to do a building job at a fixed rate. Apart from leading to little care about safety measures or the final finish of the job, the system meant that employers evaded their statutory responsibility on national health insurance, redundancy payments and payments under the Industrial Training Act. The building trades unions fought vigorously against the spread of "labour-only" work which seriously exposed workers to the real risks in the industry of sickness, injury and redundancy without the financial support of the social security schemes. Further, industrial relations deteriorated in the industry as responsible trade unionism was undermined.*

THE repeal in 1946 of the Trade Disputes Act of 1927 enabled Civil Service unions once more to affiliate to the T.U.C. and increasingly in the years that followed the T.U.C. was to become even more representative of non-manual workers.

The technological, economic and social changes of the post-war years brought many more workers into technical and non-manual jobs, and these developments were reflected in the membership of unions affiliated to the T.U.C.

With inflation and stop-go economic policies frequently discriminating against public employees, the need for additional means of influencing Government policies in order to safeguard the purchasing power of salaries and gain real increases in living standards was undoubtedly the main factor which brought more non-manual unions into membership of Congress. Two such significant affiliations were those of the National and Local Government Officers' Association, with its 350,000 members in 1965, and the first teachers' union to join the T.U.C., the Association of Teachers in Technical Institutions, in 1967.

But there were still serious problems facing many unions seeking to organise non-manual employees. As late as 1964 the British Employers' Confederation was cautioning employers against recognising unions for their non-manual staffs. Not that unions catering largely for manual workers lacked problems of union membership. Serious difficulties were faced in the building trades, for example, and by the early 1960's declining industries such as coal and railways meant heavy losses in union membership.

But on balance economic forces were running in favour of trade unions. By 1967 the membership of the T.U.C. had increased by over two million since the war and by mergers and amalgamations this larger membership was distributed among 60 fewer unions.

The trend towards amalgamations did not, however, proceed at a rapid enough rate to prevent the question of trade union structure again becoming an important issue for the T.U.C. by 1962. The jobs of different groups of workers were constantly being undermined by changes in working methods and in the use of new materials. And occasionally the T.U.C. Disputes Committee was having to resolve the demarcation disputes between unions that resulted. Gradually many trade unionists began to look for more fundamental changes in trade union structure to reflect the changes taking place in industry, as was reflected in the demand for a full scale inquiry into structure at the 1962 Congress.

The General Council after the war had renewed their own efforts to rationalise trade union structure, and working on the principles of the 1927 and 1944

*Outside Lloyds Bank in Cardiff in November, 1967, three bank girls on strike for recognition of their union, the National Union of Bank Employees,*

*distribute leaflets putting the union's case to bank customers. The T.U.C. had started an inquiry into union membership in each industry a few weeks before to*

*help in its studies of recognition problems and union structure.*

Reports on Trade Union Structure dismissed any one theory of trade unionism as ideal and encouraged union mergers where they seemed desirable.

The 1962 Congress motion which ushered in the second phase of the T.U.C.'s efforts in this direction prompted the T.U.C. General Secretary to expand what Lord Citrine had said half a century earlier.

"If structure was a function of purpose then the first question to be asked was what are we here for?" he said. That question in itself would take a year's work, he predicted, and then it would still be a long business. Indeed, it is not finished yet. A series of conferences was set in chain involving 14 groups of unions where amalgamation or closer working arrangements appeared to be sensible. These conferences are still being held. Already the rate of union structural change has been given a new impetus. In the shipbuilding industry, for example, long subject to technological and structural change, the blacksmiths, boilermakers and shipwrights amalgamated in 1963, and in printing there was increasing concentration of trade union membership with moves towards closer unity in the industry. When a further amalgamation between the Amalgamated Engineering Union and the Foundry

Workers, initiated in 1967, is completed, no less than three-quarters of the eight and three-quarter million members affiliated to the T.U.C. will be in only 17 unions.

But full employment combined with industrial change not only brought shifts in the trade union membership between different industries and occupations. There was also a shift in the balance of power within unions from national to local level which prompted a T.U.C. inquiry into the role of shop stewards and other workplace representatives. The T.U.C. report came down firmly on the shop stewards' side. "Each year these union representatives are the instruments for settling thousands of disputes quickly and suitably," it said. "Most of them do very well and both workers and management should be grateful." But "like every other representative of a union the steward is subject to its rules and bound by its objectives."

The General Council's view of the importance of the steward as a union officer emphasised the need for training to equip him to undertake his union duties. A joint statement issued by the T.U.C. and the British Employers' Confederation in 1963 supported the case for unions themselves training their officers and encouraged the expan-

sion of training of stewards during working hours by means of day-release courses.

Other people were also asking what trade unions were for: the judges, for example. A number of court judgments involving trade unions following the House of Lords' decision in Rookes v. Barnard early in 1964 threw considerable doubt over the legal right of trade unions to use their strongest bargaining weapon—the threat of strike action. But almost the first action of the new Labour Government was to pass the Trade Disputes Act which was intended to restore the position. The Act was accompanied by the setting up of the Royal Commission on Trade Unions and Employers' Associations and the T.U.C.'s Chairman and General Secretary were appointed as commissioners.

So another task fell on the T.U.C.—the writing and submission of evidence. The 70,000-word document entitled simply "Trade Unionism" sought to explain what trade unionism was about and how it worked. The evidence showed the extent to which the trade union Movement, while holding fast to its essential beliefs and basic principles, had adapted, and was continuing to adapt, its methods and its structure to the new industrial, economic, social and political conditions which had evolved particularly since 1945.

# Pay
# pause
# to
# planning

*Selwyn Lloyd on his way to the beach in Spain. When Chancellor of the Exchequer in 1961 he angered the T.U.C. by singling out wages for the full standstill treatment, but at the same time opened the talks with both sides of industry which were to lead to the foundation of the National Economic Development Council.*

FULL co-operation on economic policy with the Conservative Governments of 1951-1964 was frustrated by the reluctance of those Governments seriously to consider the use of selective economic controls except for the purpose of restraining wages during the recurring balance of payments crises. In the early 1950's the Government had favoured a policy of letting the economy run free, and using solely monetary controls like Bank Rate to influence it. In the latter half of the decade, however, even Conservative Governments became concerned to find some way of stabilising the economy if that could be done without interfering unduly with the interests of private enterprise. Similar shifts of opinion were going on elsewhere. Employers were also giving sympathetic considerations to the idea that Governments might now at least set targets for economic growth, and so provide some guide-lines for industry. At the 1960 Federation of British Industries Conference in Brighton, where the main topic for debate was "The next Five Years," there was a consensus of dissatisfaction with the rate of economic growth in Britain, which led to the recommendation that both Government and industry should consider whether it would be possible to agree on realistic forecasts for the economy for the next five years.

Eventually, in 1961, the Chancellor of the Exchequer, Mr. Selwyn Lloyd, with the backing of the Prime Minister, Mr. Harold Macmillan (whose mind had always been receptive to some of the potentialities of planning) accepted the current need for some degree of planning. Yet, in July of the same year, the Chancellor of the Exchequer imposed his famous pay pause. This was

anathema to the T.U.C., because it singled out wages for the full standstill treatment, and also because it was bound to have a particularly harsh impact upon public servants. However, Selwyn Lloyd accompanied the imposition of a pay pause with an invitation to both sides of industry to join him in considering the implications of setting targets for planned increases in output. And the General Council of the T.U.C. recognised the opportunities presented by this change in the Conservative Government's attitude.

Discussions with a view to the establishment of a National Economic Development Council continued between Government, employers and T.U.C. throughout the rest of 1961. The General Council insisted that no subject must be excluded from the prospective N.E.D.C.'s scope: it was for the Government to demonstrate that it was genuinely open to persuasion about any aspect of its policy. The General Council also reserved the right to continue to criticise publicly such of the Government's policies as they might think misguided.

Furthermore, they insisted that the trade union members of the N.E.D.C. should be in the fullest sense representative of the trade union Movement and that they should have the right and the duty to report back to the General Council of the T.U.C. The General Council were, in fact, determined that the N.E.D.C. should do practical business on behalf of Government and both sides of industry; and that under no circumstances should it become a congenial talking shop for a collection of individuals.

The National Economic Development

The National Economic Development Council at its first meeting in March, 1962. Fourth from the right is Sir Harry Douglass, then Chairman of the T.U.C. Economic Committee, and on his right are T.U.C. General Secretary George Woodcock and Lord Carron (Amalgamated Engineering Union) and under the picture, right to left, are Frank Cousins (Transport and General Workers' Union), Sidney Greene (National Union of Railwaymen) and Ron Smith (Union of Post Office Workers).

Council was fully inaugurated in March, 1962; and the T.U.C. found it re-assuring that an independent office was at the same time set up to service the work of the Council.

In accordance with the T.U.C.'s long-held view that planning ought to be concerned with particular industries and that the appropriate trade unions must be associated with all planning developments, agreement was reached towards the end of 1963 on the establish-ment of planning machinery for individual industries. The task of the Economic Development Committees—little Neddies—was to co-ordinate activities in the various industrial sectors within the requirements of the overall national economic targets.

First the T.U.C. and then, gradually, individual unions now got down to examining the details of specific economic and industrial policies. To them, now, problems of the relationships between production, productivity and employment in given industries became a matter of direct concern. And among trade unionists there was a growing awareness that a more significant development than any hitherto brought about by any change of the political Party in power, was currently taking place in trade union relationships with Government.

The T.U.C. acknowledged that stable economic growth at home was dependent upon the sound development of inter-national trade. For too long Govern-ments, to meet short-term crises in the balance of payments, had subjected the economy to stop-go policies. So in 1964 a T.U.C. statement on trade and development urged that talks in the International Monetary Fund should concentrate on establishing a new international credit-creating agency so that credit would be available to help any country to carry out the necessary economic changes that only in the long-term would correct balance of payments deficits.

When the 1964 general election returned Labour to office the trend towards economic planning was given added strength. The Department of Economic Affairs was set up to stimulate and co-ordinate economic planning and talks began immediately with the T.U.C. on Britain's first National Plan.

For the next year the E.D.C.s drew together all the facts and figures on which the plan was to be based, but the exercise was to prove of temporary and limited value, for only ten months after the Plan was published it was overtaken by the Government's massive defla-tionary measures taken to save the pound.

If anything the T.U.C.'s commitment to planning was strengthened rather than weakened by this experience, for the whole purpose of long-term plan-ning was to break out of the stop-go cycle which had characterised the British economy since the war.

Accordingly a detailed memorandum urging a much more definitive planning exercise was put to the N.E.D.C. by the T.U.C. in 1967. This memorandum advocated Government intervention and action at industry and individual firm level in order to bring about the changes necessary to achieve target growth rates. These were to be de-veloped in the T.U.C.'s first Annual Economic Review published early in 1968.

Sidney Greene, Chairman of the T.U.C. Economic Committee, leaves No. 10 Downing Street in December 1967 after a meeting with the Prime Minister, the Chancellor of the Exchequer and the Minister for Economic Affairs to discuss the T.U.C.'s first annual economic review setting out the guidelines for the next year's incomes policy.

*Harold Wilson, the Labour Party's fraternal delegate to the 1964 Trades Union Congress, makes his address shortly before he was to become Prime Minister.*

*The container revolution. Along lines supported by the T.U.C. the Government pushes ahead with plans for an integrated road and rail freight service using standard*

# In industry, trade unionists are given

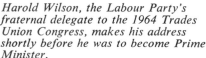

WITH THE return of the Labour Government in 1964 the trend towards tighter Government control of the economy gathered pace. The aims were to achieve more stable economic growth and to restrain the growth of incomes within what the nation could afford. Inevitably this led the Government to put pressure on both sides of industry to pursue policies in harmony with these objectives.

Trade union hopes that the Government would take a much firmer grip on the economy were raised at the 1964 Congress less than two months before the new Government was to come into office when Harold Wilson told delegates that the practical problems which arose in individual industries would not wait for years, and these problems would be dealt with by direct consultation. This, he said, would mean a real partnership—genuine consultation, not the mere presentation of a diktat.

Even before 1964, Government was seeking the advice of employers and the T.U.C. on establishing new industrial policies. For example, in the late 1950's and 1960's a whole series of bills on what is now known as labour market policy aiming to get a better deployment of the nation's manpower had been discussed in the National Joint Advisory Council to the Minister of Labour.

The Terms and Conditions of Employment Act, the Contracts of Employment Act, the Industrial Training Act, the Redundancy Payments Act were all subject to close T.U.C. scrutiny before they were ever presented to Parliament. And as the T.U.C. Annual Reports show, many of their clauses were the result of T.U.C. advocacy.

The implementation of these new laws led to a further extension of trade union participation in public administration. Taking industrial training as an example, the T.U.C. has six representatives on the Central Council which advises the Minister on the operation of the Act, and trade unions are represented on all the 21 industrial training boards established for different industries. The boards have the power to impose a levy on all firms within the industry they cover, and to pay grants to employers who provide satisfactory training.

At the same time the need for major organisational changes in many industries led Governments to establish a number of special committees of inquiry into particular industries, including shipbuilding, aircraft, and transport. The T.U.C. presented evidence to all these committees and the General Council were often able to record agreement with the advice proffered by these committees and with the subsequent action taken by Government.

Yet most of British industry was not subject to special scrutiny and was only covered by the Government's blanket arrangements for encouraging industrial policies that fitted in with national economic objectives.

The T.U.C.'s first Annual Economic Review in 1968 argued, however, that the success of Britain's economic performance was dependent to a large degree on the activities of companies which were to a substantial extent, autonomous. When it came to increasing exports, finding ways of import saving, encouraging investment to reduce regional unemployment or any other national economic objective, the nation was still very much dependent on what individual companies were prepared to do.

To make individual company policy conform more to national requirements the review sought more selective and discriminatory public financial policies

e containers which can be easily
ferred at the railhead on to road
sporters.

The Minister of Labour, Ray Gunter. On
a visit to one of the 40 Government
Training Centres which train and retrain
workers in new skills. In 1967, the centres
were turning out nearly 10,000 trainees
every year and more centres were
being planned. The vast majority of

skilled workers, however, still receive their
training on the job. To share out the
cost of this, industrial training boards
with trade union representatives levy all
employers in an industry and pay
grants to those firms providing
satisfactory training.

## ew role

which would directly favour firms whose
plans fitted in with the country's
economic objectives. As an example, it
recommended reducing the general rate
of investment grants available to all
firms by as much as a half, and then
distributing the grants selectively to
firms who either met the requirements
of different regions or pursued policies

which would boost exports, save imports
or add to national economic advantage
in some other way.

Equally important in the review was a
demand for trade unions to be able to
put their view of industrial policy not
only in the National Economic Development Council and Economic Develop-

ment Committees, but in each individual
company and plant. As workers' jobs as
well as their wages were always liable to
be affected by measures designed to
increase industrial efficiency, the review
argued that trade unions should be
closely involved in making company
policy, particularly in planning how
manpower was to be used effectively.

In July, 1967, George
Woodcock, T.U.C. General
Secretary, signs the
T.U.C./C.B.I. joint
initiative on productivity.
Waiting to sign are (left to
right) John Davies,
Director General C.B.I.,
Sir Harry Douglass,
Chairman T.U.C. General
Council, Sir Stephen
Brown, Chairman C.B.I.
Grand Council.

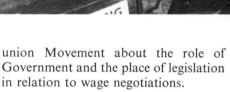

*The Right Hon. George Brown, Secretary of State for Economic Affairs and Lord Collison, chairman of the General Council after signing the Joint Statement on Intent on Productivity, Prices and Incomes in December 1964. The Joint Statement marked a significant change in the approach of all three bodies to these matters; from now on they were to set out to co-operate in tackling the prickly issues involved.*

# The Government puts on the pressure for a prices and income policy

ATTEMPTS by the T.U.C. to get an incomes, prices and productivity policy did not begin with the return of the Labour Government in 1964—far from it. But what the new Government did do was to put pressure on trade unionists to turn their resolutions into practical policies.

Only three months after the Government took office the first tangible signs of progress emerged with the signing of the Joint Statement of Intent on Productivity, Prices and Incomes by representatives of the T.U.C., the employers and the Government. This tripartite approach was to continue throughout the next two years as the Minister for Economic Affairs, Mr. George Brown, kept the pressure on to develop the policy.

Machinery for administering the policy, including the setting up of the National Board for Prices and Incomes, and the criteria for judging the justification for wage and prices increases quickly followed the Statement of Intent and were approved by a special Conference of Union Executives called by the T.U.C. in April 1965.

Later in the same year the difference of view between the Government and the T.U.C. over the question of enforcement of incomes policy was revealed when the Government, under pressure to correct the balance of payments, requested the T.U.C.'s support for legislation containing penalties for recalcitrants who would not co-operate with the majority in operating the policy.

Meanwhile, the T.U.C. was making its own arrangements for administering its incomes policy. The 1965 Congress agreed that unions should notify their wage claims for review in light of the policy, and an Incomes Policy Committee of the General Council was set up in the following month.

Renewed pressure on the pound, however, led to the Government calling for a standstill on prices and incomes during 1966 and the T.U.C. reluctantly acquiesced in the Government's decision. The Prices and Incomes Bill which had been introduced earlier was strengthened for a twelve month period but the point when the Government and the T.U.C. were to diverge over the administration of the policy was close. By November 1966 the T.U.C. had produced its own plans for the long-term development of a voluntary incomes policy. The T.U.C.'s proposals for building the voluntary policy were for an annual conference of union executives to discuss a T.U.C. report on the economic situation, which would set out the considerations according to which the T.U.C. Incomes Policy Committee would review wage claims in the following year. The report would be the subject of close and detailed consultation between the T.U.C. and the Government and the C.B.I. but it would be "a trade union view of the situation and its requirements, presented by trade unionists to trade unionists".

In addition, the T.U.C. would open discussions with the C.B.I. about minimum wages and working conditions, and would seek to co-ordinate trade union wage claims so that they could be presented simultaneously.

The Report, which was approved by a Conference of Union Executives in 1967, also clarified the views of the trade union Movement about the role of Government and the place of legislation in relation to wage negotiations.

"It is in the interests of trade unions, of the community at large and of the Government itself that Government interference in wage and salary negotiations should be kept to a minimum," it said. "Even more important, attempts at interference—particularly by legislation—in this field could only strengthen authoritarian tendencies and weaken the principle of voluntary association which is the mainstay of British democracy."

The first steps in this new approach to incomes policy were taken with publication of the T.U.C. first Annual Economic Review early in 1968 and discussed on the previous page.

Yet incomes policy could not carry the whole burden of removing the inequalities of incomes: social security provisions had a part to play. Over the years the General Council had argued the case for improving the basic national insurance rate of benefits and family allowances; the improvements in these directions since, 1964 were welcomed. However, according to an official inquiry in 1966 the earnings of a significant number of workers with families were below subsistence level and many other voices were joining the T.U.C. in demanding a substantial increase in family allowances with offsetting changes in income tax.

The T.U.C. Review affirmed that incomes policy had a positive part to play in securing full employment, in enabling real wages to grow at a faster rate and in promoting the claims of the less well-off sections of the community.

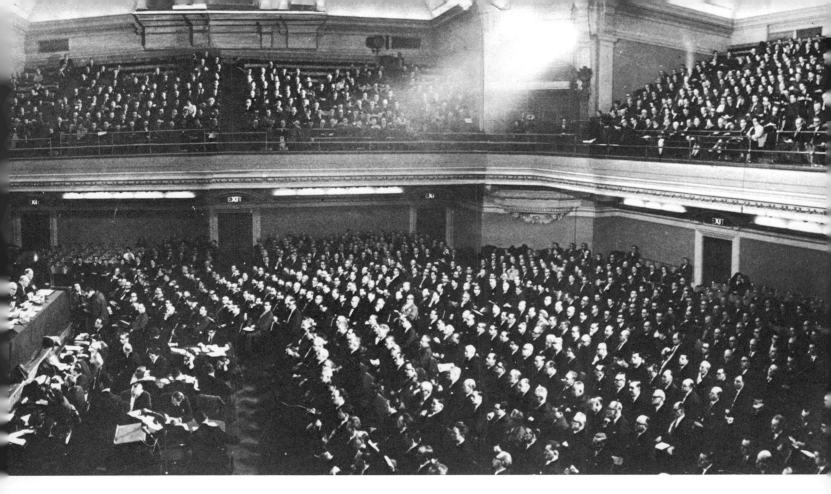

*The scene at Central Hall, Westminster, in March, 1967, when the Conference of Union Executives approved by an overwhelming majority the T.U.C.'s proposals for a voluntary incomes policy.*

# Overseas the T.U.C. gives advice and seeks to learn

*Two T.U.C. advisers in the home of the President of the Northern Rhodesian African Miners' Union in 1955 during the 58-day strike by the union against the exclusion of Africans from skilled jobs in the copper-mining industry.*

*A delegation of trade unionists from the Soviet Union being greeted on arrival by the T.U.C. General Secretary, George Woodcock, and Assistant General Secretary Victor Feather, at London Airport. Led by Mr. Peter Pimenov, General Secretary of the Soviet A.U.C.C.T.U., the delegation spent two weeks in Britain in September, 1967.*

AFTER the war the T.U.C. built up its service of advice and practical aid to unions in developing countries requesting help, and the service was expanded in the 1950's. Later in the period the General Council began a series of study visits to Sweden, Israel and West Germany; and as the cold war became less intense the T.U.C. was able to send full delegations to Yugoslavia and the Soviet Union, with a return visit by the Russians in 1967, without damaging friendly relations elsewhere. The T.U.C. continued mainly to base its international policies of union co-operation on the International Confederation of Free Trade Unions, and the visits to countries in the Communist World Federation of Trade Unions were organised strictly on the understanding that their object was to study the purposes and functions of trade unions in different social systems.

AS THE T.U.C. took on increasing responsibilities, the General Council had at times to reinforce the authority given to them by union delegates at the annual Congress by seeking the explicit support of the governing bodies of affiliated unions—their national executive committees. For example, to secure authority to call unions out on strike in 1926, the General Council had convened a Conference of Executives; and they did so on a number of occasions to discuss and decide policies of wage restraint in the early post-war period. The growing acceptance by governments of the T.U.C.'s view that they must intervene more extensively and systematically in regulating the nation's economic affairs meant that the General Council, in discussions with the Government, had to have sufficient authority to commit the trade union Movement.

The development of the T.U.C.'s role in relation to incomes policy from 1965 on necessitated the General Council providing guidance to unions generally on bargaining strategy as well as to unions individually on specific wage claims. This development inevitably involved the T.U.C. more directly and more frequently with what had hitherto been the exclusively domestic concern of unions, and a conference at which executives could meet to formulate policy became an annual requirement.

The T.U.C.'s own executive—its General Council—also had to reflect the shifts in employment that had led to changes in the membership of different unions, if they were to continue to represent effectively and to command the support of member unions. Five times since the war the basis of union representation in the General Council was changed, particularly to reflect more adequately within the T.U.C. the growth of trade union membership among public employees, technicians and other non-manual workers. And further proposals for reform were put forward early in 1968 for consideration by the 100th Trades Union Congress.

At the same time as the General Council, with the backing of Congress and the Conference of Executives, were being called upon to act for the Movement at large the T.U.C.'s policies increasingly called for action by every union and by union representatives in each workplace. Thus, in demanding that governments should act in partnership with the trade union Movement to plan for full employment and rising living standards, trade unionists themselves have had to accept new and wider responsibilities.

In a statement presented to Congress in 1963 on economic development and planning the General Council declared that the need to relate trade union functions to their participation in planning necessitated a re-appraisal of T.U.C. and trade union research and communications, union bargaining methods and union structure and organisation. This need was underlined in the 1968 T.U.C. Economic Review which demanded not only influence in determining national planning targets but also the acceptance by employers of union co-operation in achieving such objectives through participation in the development of policy at company and plant level.

The complexity of the tasks confronting the Movement has already required, for example, that the T.U.C. should undertake extensive detailed research into the issues affecting economic growth and the effects on workpeople of specific industrial changes. Since the effectiveness of the Movement's policies depends upon unions being able to interpret T.U.C. policies in the light of the special circumstances facing their own members in many different jobs, trade union influence on Economic Development Committees, Industrial Training Boards and on the policies of individual companies is increasingly dependent upon union representatives being backed up effectively by their own unions' research and technical departments.

*Studying the debates and decisions of the 1967 Congress in the T.U.C. information broadsheet "Labour".*

*In the T.U.C. Training College, which takes 700 full-time and voluntary union officers every year as students, the T.U.C.'s Medical Adviser takes a class on the health hazards of dust in industry. To discover more precisely the effects of work and working conditions on health the T.U.C. decided in 1967 to set up an Institute of Occupational Health at the London School of Hygiene and Tropical Medicine.*

The T.U.C. Education Service has come a long way to meet the changing needs of trade unions for educational and training services since the first T.U.C. Summer Schools were held in 1929. Initially, the service aimed to inform trade unionists of the policies of the T.U.C. and the circumstances surrounding them, but with the increasing responsibilities of trade unions in industry and with public authorities concerned with industry and the social services, union training became an urgent necessity. This need was foreseen during the war when the General Council included a Training College in their plans for the T.U.C.'s new headquarters. The series of T.U.C. short, full-time training courses began in 1947 and developed rapidly after the opening of the T.U.C. Training College in 1957.

Increasingly unions developed their own training schemes, and by 1958 the Electrical Trades Union and the General and Municipal Workers had established their own Colleges. But most unions continued to rely mainly upon workers' educational bodies for their educational services. The T.U.C. assumed responsibility for such services in 1962. The new T.U.C. Education Service included an extensive range of postal courses freely available to all union members, and the provision of weekend, day-release and evening courses in the regions designed to meet the needs of shop stewards and other local union officers.

To assist unions in keeping their members informed on T.U.C. affairs the General Council decided in 1965 to change the format of its journal "Labour" and to publish it as a broadsheet free of charge to unions for circulation to their branches. But at the same time trade unionists were increasingly able to learn a good deal about policies of the Movement through press and television, assisted by the T.U.C.'s services to the press and particularly to the industrial correspondents of newspapers and of the broadcasting authorities.

The expanding work of the T.U.C. at home and abroad meant that affiliation fees which stood at 2½d. a member a year in 1945, were to go up sevenfold by 1968. The 1967 Congress approved an increase in contributions to enable the T.U.C. Centenary to be marked by the establishment of the T.U.C. Institute of Occupational Health and by other appropriate activities and also to finance a general expansion of T.U.C. services at the outset of the T.U.C.'s second century.

*Looking down on the platform at the 99th Trades Union Congress from left to right, Lord Carron, George Lowthian, Fred Hayday, Joe O'Hagan, Sir Harry Douglass, George Woodcock, Victor Feather, Wilf Beard, Lord Collison.*

*Lord Wright, General Secretary of the Amalgamated Weavers' Association, Chairman of the 1967-68 T.U.C. General Council and President of the Centenary Congress.*

# Trade Unions affiliated to the TUC March 1968

Actors' Equity Association, British
Agricultural Workers, National Union of
Asphalt Workers, Amalgamated Union of
Bakers' Union
Bakers and Allied Workers, Scottish Union of
Bakers' Union, London Jewish
Bank Employees, National Union of
Basket, Cane, Wicker and Fibre Furniture Makers of Great Britain and Ireland, The National Union of
Beamers, Twisters and Drawers (Hand and Machine), Amalgamated Association of
Blastfurnacemen, Ore Miners, Coke Workers, and Kindred Trades, The National Union of
Blind and Disabled, The National League of the
Boilermakers, Shipwrights, Blacksmiths and Structural Workers, Amalgamated Society of
Boot & Shoe Operatives, National Union of
Boot, Shoe and Slipper Operatives, Rossendale Union of
British Air Line Pilots' Association
Broadcasting Staff, Association of
Brushmakers, National Society of
Building Technicians, Association of
Building Trade Workers of Great Britain and Ireland, Amalgamated Union of
Card, Blowing and Ring Room Operatives, National Association of
Card Setting Machine Tenters' Society
Carpet Trade Union, Northern
Chain Makers and Strikers' Association
Chemical Workers' Union
Cigarette Machine Operators' Society
Cinematograph, Television and Allied Technicians, Association of
Civil Service Clerical Association
Civil Service Union
Clerical and Administrative Workers' Union
Cloth Pressers' Society
Colliery Overmen, Deputies and Shotfirers, National Association of
Commercial Motormen's Union, Scottish
Commercial Travellers, National Union of
Constructional Engineering Union
Co-operative Officials, National Union of
Coopers' Federation of Great Britain and Ireland
County Court Officers' Association
Customs and Excise Federation
Customs and Excise Preventive Staff Association
Domestic Appliance and General Metal Workers, National Union of
Draughtsmen's and Allied Technicians' Association
Dyers, Bleachers and Textile Workers, National Union of
Electrical Power Engineers' Association
Electrical Trades Union
Engineering Union, Amalgamated
Engineer Surveyors' Association
Engineers' and Firemen's Union, Grimsby Steam and Diesel Fishing Vessels
Engravers, United Society of
Felt Hatters and Allied Workers, Amalgamated
Felt Hat Trimmers, Wool Formers and Allied Workers, Amalgamated
File Trades, Sheffield Amalgamated Union of
Film Artists' Association, The
Fire Brigades Union
Foundry Workers, Amalgamated Union of
French Polishers' Society, United
Funeral and Cemetery Workers, National Union of
Furniture Trade Operatives, National Union of
General and Municipal Workers, National Union of
Glass Bevellers and Kindred Trades Society, Midland
Glovers and Leather Workers, National Union of
Gold, Silver and Allied Trades, National Union of
Goldsmiths, Jewellers and Kindred Trades, The Society of
Graphical and Allied Trades, Society of
Graphical Association, National
Greater London Council Staff Association
Healders and Twisters' Trade and Friendly Society, Huddersfield
Health Service Employees, Confederation of
Health Visitors' Association
Hosiery Finishers' Association, Nottingham and District
Hosiery and Knitwear Workers, National Union of
Hosiery Trimmers' Association, Leicester and Leicestershire
Inland Revenue Staff Federation
Insurance Officials, Guild of
Insurance Workers, National Union of
Iron and Steel Trades Confederation
Iron, Steel and Wood Barge Builders' and Helpers' Association
Journalists, National Union of
Jute, Flax and Kindred Textile Operatives, Union of
Lace Makers and Textile Workers, Amalgamated Society of Operative
Laminated and Coil Spring Workers' Union

Leather Workers, Amalgamated Society of
Leather Workers, National Union of
Lithographic Artists, Designers, Engravers and Process Workers, Society of
Lithographic Printers, The Amalgamated Society of
Lock and Metal Workers, National Union of
Locomotive Engineers and Firemen, Associated Society of
Loom Overlookers, the General Union of Associations of
Machine Calico Printers, Trade Society of
Managers and Overlookers' Society
Medical Practitioners' Union
Merchant Navy and Air Line Officers' Association
Metal Mechanics, National Society of
Metalworkers' Society, Associated
Military and Orchestral Musical Instrument Makers' Trade Society
Mineworkers, National Union of
Ministry of Labour Staff Association
Musicians' Union
National Coal Board Labour Staff Association
National and Local Government Officers' Association
Painters and Decorators, Amalgamated Society of
Patternmakers' Association, United
Plasterers, The National Association of Operative
Plumbing Trades Union
Post Office Management Staffs, Association of
Post Office Engineering Union
Post Office Workers, Union of
Pottery Workers, National Society of
Power Loom Carpet Weavers and Textile Workers' Association
Power Loom Overlookers, Yorkshire Association of
Power Loom Tenters, Scottish Union of
Print Block Roller and Stamp Cutters' Society
Prison Officers' Association
Process and General Workers' Union
Professional Footballers' and Trainers' Association
Public Employees, National Union of
Radio Officers' Union
Railwaymen, National Union of
Retail Book, Stationery and Allied Trades Employees' Association
Roll Turners' Trade Society, British
Rubber Workers of Great Britain, The United
Sailmakers, Amalgamated Union of
Salt, Chemical and Industrial General Workers, Union of
Sawmakers' Protection Society, Sheffield
Scalemakers, National Union of
Scientific, Technical and Managerial Staffs, The Association of
Screw, Nut, Bolt and Rivet Trade Society
Seamen, National Union of
Sheet Metal Workers, Coppersmiths and Heating and Domestic Engineers, National Union of
Sheet Metal Workers' Society, Birmingham and Midland
Shop, Distributive and Allied Workers, Union of
Shuttlemakers, Society of
Sign and Display Trades Union
Slaters, Tilers and Roofing Operatives' Society, Amalgamated
Spinners and Twiners, Amalgamated Association of Operative Cotton
Spring Trapmakers' Society
Tailors and Garment Workers, National Union of
Teachers in Technical Institutions, Association of
Technical Civil Servants, Society of
Telecommunication Engineers, Society of
Textile Craftsmen, Yorkshire Society of
Textile Dayman's and Cloth Pattern Makers' Association
Textile Warehousemen, Amalgamated
Textile Workers and Kindred Trades, Amalgamated Society of
Theatrical and Kine Employees, The National Association of
Tobacco Workers' Union, The
Transport and General Workers' Union
Transport Salaried Staffs' Association
Transport Union, The United Road
Typographical Association
Vehicle Builders, National Union of
Wall Paper Workers' Union
Warpdressers, Twisters and Kindred Trades Associations, Leeds and District
Water Works Employees, National Union of
Watermen, Lightermen, Tugmen and Bargemen's Union
Waterproof Garment Workers' Trade Union, The
Weavers' Association, Amalgamated
Weavers and Woollen Textile Workers' Association, Saddleworth and District
Wire Drawers and Kindred Workers, The Amalgamated Society of
Wood-cutting Machinists, Amalgamated Society of
Woodworkers, Amalgamated Society of
Wool Shear Workers' Trade Union, Sheffield
Wool Sorters' Society, National
Writers' Guild of Great Britain

# Members of the Parliamentary Committee from 1868 and of the General Council from 1921

*Since the election of the General Council in 1921 the dates given are of the year of the Congress at which appointment was made, or in the event of election to fill a casual vacancy, the year in which it took place.*

Allan, W 1871–4.
Allen, A W 1962–7.
Allen, W P 1940–7.
Anderson, J 1892.
Anderson, W C 1965–7.
Arch, J 1874, 1876.
Arrandale, M 1908–12.
Baddeley, Winifred 1963–7.
Basnett, D 1966–7.
Bagnall, G H 1939–47.
Bailey, A W 1869, 1872, 1874, 1876–86.
Ball, J M 1877–80.
Barnes, G N 1906–7.
Bartlett, C 1948–62.
Battersby, J 1876.
Baty, J G 1947–54.
Beard, J 1920–34.
Beard, W B 1947–66.
Bell, J 1937–45.
Bell, J N 1921–22.
Bell, R 1899, 1902–9.
Benstead, J 1944–7.
Berry, H 1935–7.
*Bevin, E 1925–40.
Birch, J A 1949–61.
Birtwistle, T 1877–89, 1891.
Boa, A 1874.
*Bondfield, Margaret 1917–23, 1925–9.
Boothman, H 1919–35.
Bostock, F 1947.
Bothwell, J G 1963–7.
Bowen, J W 1921–7.
Bowerman, C W 1897–1911.
Bowman, J 1946–9.
Boyd, J M 1967.
Bramley, F 1916–17.
Briginshaw, R W 1965–7.
Broadhurst, H 1874–89, 1893–4.
Bromley, J 1921–35.
Brown, J 1936–45.
Brown, W 1875.
Bullock, H 1937–50.
Burnett, J 1876–85.
Burns, J 1890, 1893–4.
Burrows, A W 1947–8.
Bussey, E W 1941–6.
Campbell, J 1953–7.
Callighan, A 1945–7.
Cannon, L 1965–7.
Carron, W J 1954–67.
Chandler, F 1895–9, 1901–3, 1905–10, 1916.
Chester, G 1937–48.
Collindridge, F 1961–2.
Collison, H 1953–67.
Conley, A 1921–48.
Cook, A J 1927–31.
Cooper, B 1907–8.
Cooper, J 1959–67.
Cotter, J 1923–4.
Coulson, E 1869.
†Cousins, F 1956–64, 1966–7.
Cowey, E 1893–1903.
Cramp, C T 1929–32.
Crawford, J 1949–56.
Crawford, Joseph 1960–7.
Crawford, W 1878–80, 1882–9.
Cummings, D C 1901–8.
Dann, A C 1945–52.
Davenport, J 1921, 1924–33.
Davis, W J 1881–3, 1896–1901, 1903–20.

Davies, D H 1967.
Deakin, A 1940–54.
Dewhurst, C D 1868.
Douglass, H 1953–66.
Dronfield, W H 1868.
Dukes, C 1934–46.
Eastwood, H 1948.
Eccles, T 1949–58.
Edwards, E 1931–46.
Edwards, G 1912.
Elvin, H H 1925–39.
Emery, H 1909–11.
Evans, A 1911–15.
Evans, L 1945–52.
Evans, W J 1960–2.
Farthing, W J 1935–43.
Fawcett, L 1940–51.
Fenwick, C 1890–3.
Ferguson, G 1895.
Figgins, J B 1947–52.
Findlay, A A H 1921–40.
Fitzpatrick, J 1878.
Flynn, T A 1916–17.
Ford, S W G 1963–7.
Forden, L 1958–65.
Forshaw, W 1933–4.
Gallie, C N 1940–6.
Geddes, C J 1946–56.
Gibson, G 1928–47.
Gill, A H 1903–7, 1913–14.
Godwin, Anne 1949–62.
Gosling, H 1908–23.
Green, G. F. 1960–2.
Greene, S F 1957–67.
Greenhall, T 1918.
Griffiths, A E 1963–7.
Guile, D 1871–5.
Hall, E 1954–9.
Hall, F 1917.
Halliday, T 1875–6.
Hallsworth, J 1926–46.
Hallworth, A 1955–9.
Hancock, Florence 1935–57.
Handley, R C 1938–9.
Harford, E 1887–92, 1894–7.
Harrison, H N 1937–47.
Haslam, J 1904–12.
Hayday, A 1922–36.
Hayday, F 1950–67.
Haynes, E 1964–7.
Hewitt, H 1952–63.
Heywood, W L 1948–56.
Hicks, G 1921–40.
Hill, A L 1955–7.
Hill, E J 1948–64.
Hill, J 1909–35.
Hill, J C 1959.
Hill, S 1963–7.
Hindle, J 1930–6.
Hobson, C 1900–1.
Hodge, J 1892–3, 1895.
Hodgson, M 1936–47.
Hogarth, W 1962–7.
Holmes, D 1892–1900, 1902–3.
Holmes, W 1928–44.
Hornidge, W B 1899–1907.
Houghton, D 1952–9.
Howell, G 1869–75.
Hudson, W 1898.
Inglis, J 1877–85, 1887–9, 1891.
Inskip, W 1887–98.
*Isaacs, G A 1932–45.
Jack, J M 1884–8, 1890, 1892–6.
Jackson, T 1967.

Jarman, C 1942–6.
Jenkins, H 1909–17.
Jones, J 1934–8.
Jones, J. W. 1967.
Jones, L 1872.
Jones, R J 1946–56.
Jones, R T 1921–32.
Jones, W E 1950–9.
Judson, E 1917.
Kane, J 1869, 1872–3, 1875.
Kaylor, J 1938–42.
Kean, W 1921–45.
Kelly, G D 1871, 1883, 1887, 1890–1.
Knight, R 1875–82, 1896–1900.
Lawther, W 1935–53.
Leatherland, W H 1883.
Lee, P 1933.
Leicester, J 1871.
Leslie, J 1925.
Loughlin, Anne 1929–52.
Lowthian, G H 1952–67.
Macdonald, A 1871–4.
Marchbank, J 1924, 1933–42.
Martin, A 1960–7.
Matkin, W 1871, 1890–1, 1911–15.
Mawdsley, J. 1882, 1884–9, 1891–6.
McAndrews, A 1949–54.
McCullough, Ellen 1958–62.
McDermott, J F 1949–57.
McGarvey, D 1965–7.
McGurk, J 1932.
Mitchell, I H 1897.
Moore, J H 1922–3.
Mosses, W 1907–11, 1913–7.
Mottershead, T 1874.
Mullin, W 1897, 1902, 1908–12, 1915.
Murchie, J S 1883–6, 1888.
Murnin, H 1921.
Naesmith, A 1945–52.
Newton, J E 1953–67.
Nicholas, H R 1965–6.
O'Brien, T 1940–67.
Odger, G 1872–6.
Ogden, J W 1911–29.
O'Hagan, J 1953–66.
Onions, A 1917–18.
Openshaw, R 1948–56.
Owen, J 1948–52.
Owen, W 1873.
Papworth, A F 1944–8.
Patterson, C Marie 1963–7.
Patterson, W 1881–2.
Paynter, W 1960.
Peel, J A 1966–7.
Pickard, B 1890.
Plackett, T 1873.
Plant, C T H 1963–7.
Poole, L 1957–8.
Potter, G 1868–9, 1872.
Poulton, E L 1917–29.
Prior, J D 1871, 1875–80.
Pugh, A 1920–35.
Purcell, A A 1919–27.
Quaile, Mary 1923–5.
Richards, T 1925–31.
Roberts, A 1940–62.
Roberts, A 1967.
Robinson, S A 1959–67.
Rolley, W 1874–6.
Rowan, J 1921–34.

Scott, J 1961.
Seddon, J A 1908–15.
Sedgwick, G 1884–5.
Sexton, J 1900–5, 1907, 1909–21.
Shackleton, D J 1904–10.
Sharp, L 1957–65.
Shaw, A 1929–38.
Sheldon, R 1884.
Sherwood, W 1934–6.
Shipton, G 1875–81, 1883, 1885–9.
Shirkie, R 1918.
Shorrocks, P. 1868, 1873.
Skinner, H 1915, 1917–20, 1921–31.
Slatter, H 1877–89.
Smillie, R 1917, 1920–6.
Smith, A 1913–5, 1921.
Smith, G F 1959–67.
Smith, H 1913–6, 1922–4, 1931.
Smith, R 1957–66.
Smith, T 1877.
Spackman, E W 1945–6.
Spence, W R 1931–41.
Squance, W J R 1936–9.
Steadman, W C 1899–1910.
Stott, W 1936–9.
Stuart-Bunning, G H 1916–20.
Swales, A B 1919–34.
Swift, J 1886, 1889.
Swindell, B 1962–5.
Tanner, J 1943–53.
Tallon, W M 1957–66.
Thomas, J H 1917–23, 1925–8.
Thomson, G W 1935–47.
Thorne, W 1894–1933.
Thorneycroft, G B 1948–52.
Threlfall, T 1891.
Tiffin, A E 1955.
Tillett, B 1892–4, 1921–31.
Townley, W R 1930–6.
Turner, B 1921–8.
Turner, J 1921–4.
Uttley, S 1886, 1890.
Varley, Julia 1921–5, 1926–34.
Walkden, A G 1921–35.
Walker, R B 1917–27.
Watson, T 1908.
Walsh, B 1950, 1957–9.
Webber, W J P 1953–62.
Wilkie, A 1890, 1895–1902, 1904–8.
Wilkinson, J 1868.
Williams, J B 1907–1910, 1912–15, 1917–20, 1921–4.
Williams, J E 1910–16.
Williams, R W 1938–46.
Williamson, T 1947–61.
Willis, R 1947–64.
Wilson, J 1890–2.
Wilson, J H 1889–97, 1918.
Wolstencroft, F 1928–48.
Wood, W 1936–7.
Wood, W H 1868.
Woods, S 1894–1904.
Wright, L T 1953–67.
Yates, T 1947–60.

*Resigned on appointment as Minister of Labour.
†Resigned on appointment as Minister of Technology.

# Acknowledgements

The production of this book would not have been possible without the co-operation and assistance of the *Radio Times Hulton Picture Library,* and in particular their librarian, Miss Daphne Moss, in lending to the T.U.C. the majority of the pictures which appear in this volume. The T.U.C. is also grateful to the following for permitting the use of pictorial material reproduced on the following pages:

Barratt's Ltd.
**50 80** (*top*)

British Rail
**148-149**

Brown Bros., New York
**38** (*bottom*) **56** (*top left*) and **57** (*top right*)

Camera Press
**68** (*bottom*) **71 141** (*bottom right*)

Central Office of Information
**149** (*top right*)

Glasgow Herald
**103**

Imperial War Museum
**115** (*top*)

International Illustration Bureau
—Amsterdam
**92** (*top*)

Keystone Press
**125** (*top right*) **128** (*bottom*) **138-139**

John Laing & Sons Ltd.
**144**

London Express
**97 127** (*bottom*) **132-133**

Mansell Collection
**38** (*top left*) **53** (*bottom right*)

Tony Moore
**119**

Press Association
**54** (*bottom*) **59 73 151** (*bottom*)

Sport and General
**100 108**

Steel, Peech & Tozer
**135**

Syndication International
**74** (*middle*) **142** (*bottom*) **147**

The Guardian
**126**

The Sun
**60** (*top right*) **62 65 88** (*top*) **102 114** (*bottom*)
**116 127** (*middle top*) **129** (*bottom*) **134** (*bottom*)
**141** (*top*) **148 153** (*bottom*)

The Times
**115** (*bottom*) **142-143 146-147 149** (*bottom*)
**150 151** (*top*) **153** (*top*)

Thomson Newspapers Limited
**90 91 104 122** (*bottom*) **137** (*top*) **145**

Transport and General Workers' Union
**43 109** (*top*) **143** (*bottom*)

Union of Shop, Distributors and Allied
 Workers
**35** (*bottom*)

United Press International
**146** (*left*)

Walter Hood
**151** (*middle*)

Trades Union Congress

The following pictures were drawn from the files of the T.U.C.:

**9 10 13 15 16** (*top group*) **20** (*top left*) **42 47**
**61 74** (*top*) **75 80** (*bottom*) **86 88** (*bottom*)
**92** (*bottom*) **100** (*top*) **105 109** (*bottom*) **110**
**114** (*top*) **124 128** (*top*) **130-131** (*middle*)
**134** (*top*) **139** (*bottom right*) **152**

*End papers: Farm labourers lockout, Manchester, July, 1874 (Radio Times Hulton Picture Library)*

Every care has been taken to record the source of pictures used in this book. Many of the pictures have been taken, however, from the T.U.C.'s collection of photographs and in some cases their origin is not known.

The Editor is indebted to the late Sidney and Beatrice Webb; Clegg, Fox and Thompson; the late G. D. H. Cole; B. C. Roberts; Henry Pelling and many other historians of the trade union Movement on whose scholarship he has unashamedly drawn, and the T.U.C. gratefully acknowledges permission to quote from the following published works:

Musson, A. E.
The Congress of 1868
London. T.U.C. 1955

Brown, E. H. Phelps
The Growth of British Industrial Relations
London. Macmillan, 1959

Bullock, Alan
The Life and Times of Ernest Bevin
London. Heinemann, 1960

Hutt, A.
Post-War History of the British
Working Class
London. Gollancz, 1937

Pelling, Henry
History of British Trade Unionism
London. Penguin, 1963

Cole, G. D. H.
An Introduction to Trade Unionism
London. George Allen and Unwin, 1953

Roberts, B. C.
The Trades Union Congress, 1868-1921
London. George Allen and Unwin, 1958

Cole, G. D. H. and Postgate, Raymond
The Common People 1746-1946
London. Methuen, 1938

Citrine, Lord
Men and Work
London. Hutchinson, 1964

Webb, Sidney and Beatrice
The History of Trade Unionism
London. Longmans Green, 1950
(Quotes by permission of The Passfield Trust)

Pike, Edgar Royston
Human Documents of the Industrial
Revolution in Britain
London. Allen and Unwin, 1966

Arnott, R. Page
Trade Unions a New Model
I.L.P. pamphlet, 1919

# Index